W9-DJD-285

Betty Crocker's
ONE-DISH
MAIN MEALS

PRENTICE HALL

NEW YORK LONDON TORONTO SYDNEY TOKYO SINGAPORE

PRENTICE HALL
15 Columbus Circle
New York, New York 10023

Copyright © 1994 by General Mills, Inc., Minneapolis, Minnesota

All rights reserved,
including the right of reproduction
in whole or in part in any form.

PRENTICE HALL is a registered trademark and colophon is a trademark of Prentice-Hall, Inc.

BETTY CROCKER and Bisquick are registered trademarks of General Mills, Inc.

Library of Congress Cataloging-in-Publication Data
Crocker, Betty.
   [One-dish main meals]
   Betty Crocker's One-dish main meals.
     p.   cm.
   Includes index.
   ISBN 0-671-88331-3
   1. Entrées (Cookery) I. Title. II. Title: One-dish main meals.
TX740.C72 1994
641.8'2—dc20   93-6073
                                         CIP

GENERAL MILLS, INC.

Betty Crocker Food and Publications Center
       Director, Marcia Copeland
       Editor, Karen Couné
       Recipe Development, Sandra Granseth, Phyllis Kral
       Food Stylists, Cindy Lund, Katie W. McElroy
Nutrition Department
       Nutritionist, Elyse A. Cohen, M.S.
Photographic Services
       Photographer, Nanci Doonan Dixon

Designed by Levavi & Levavi

Manufactured in the United States of America

10 9 8 7 6 5 4 3 2 1

First Edition

Cover: Four-Cheese and Vegetable Lasagne (page 97); Stir-fried Beef and Vegetables with Linguine (page 6)

CONTENTS

INTRODUCTION

What could be easier than dinner in just one dish? Nothing! That's why we created this collection of enticing and varied meals that are complete in one dish. We are all scrambling for ways to make the most of the free time that we have, and these delicious, no-fuss dinners are the perfect way to minimize time in the kitchen.

Looking for speedy skillet dishes? Then you'll love Stir-fried Beef with Vegetables and Linguine, Sloppy Joe Skillet Dinner, Polynesian Ham and Rice, and the other meals-in-a-flash in Chapter 1. And on cold nights you can turn to Chaper 2 for Stews, Chiles and Soups and make heartening Beef Stew with Thyme Dumplings, Turkey Chile Mole or Golden Peanut Soup.

When time is at a premium, casseroles and pot pies are welcome, as you can put them in the oven and go about your business. You'll be delighted with Lamb and Lentil Casserole, Seafood Jambalaya Bake and Reuben Pot Pie. And pizza is always popular, especially with a home-made crust. Try Mexican Pan Pizza or Deep-dish Turkey Pizza for a one-dish dinner that will delight the whole family.

One-dish salads, whether hot or cold, are always a pleasure. If you are looking for a warm salad, Beef-Potato Salad or Warm Spinach Salad will fill the bill, while Citrus Shrimp Salad and Italian Bread Salad are refreshing cold salads.

And, for those times when you'd like to make something extra to round out your meal, we have included great recipes for tasty muffins and biscuits, quick breads, easy salads and speedy bread fix-ups.

We know you'll appreciate the convenience and variety of these one-dish recipes, that will help to get dinner on the table without lots of fuss, but still give you lots of great taste.

The Betty Crocker Editors

STIR-FRIES AND SKILLET DISHES

Beef and Tomato Stir-fry

2 ounces cellophane noodles, cut into pieces
1 pound beef top round steak
1 teaspoon cornstarch
½ cup beef broth
½ cup cold water
1 tablespoon cornstarch
3 tablespoons steak sauce
1 teaspoon sugar
1 tablespoon vegetable oil
2 teaspoons finely chopped gingerroot or 1 teaspoon ground ginger
1 tablespoon vegetable oil
1½ cups sliced zucchini
1 large onion, cut into thin wedges
2 medium tomatoes, cut into thin wedges

Soak cellophane noodles 15 minutes in enough warm water to cover; drain. Trim fat from beef steak. Cut beef with grain into 2-inch strips; cut strips across grain into ⅛-inch slices. (For ease in cutting, partially freeze beef about 1½ hours.) Toss beef and 1 teaspoon cornstarch. Mix broth, water, 1 tablespoon cornstarch, the steak sauce and sugar.

Heat wok or 12-inch skillet until very hot. Add 1 tablespoon oil to wok; rotate wok to coat side. Add beef and gingerroot; stir-fry about 3 minutes or until beef is brown. Remove beef mixture from wok.

Add 1 tablespoon oil to wok; rotate wok to coat side. Add zucchini and onion; stir-fry about 4 minutes or until vegetables are crisp-tender. Stir in broth mixture. Cook and stir about 1 minute or until thickened. Stir in beef mixture, cellophane noodles and tomatoes. Cook about 1 minute or until heated through. *4 servings.*

Nutrition Information Per Serving

1 serving		% of U.S. RDA	
Calories	275	Vitamin A	6%
Protein, g	30	Vitamin C	10%
Carbohydrate, g	22	Calcium	2%
Dietary fiber, g	3	Iron	20%
Fat, g	9		
Cholesterol, mg	75		
Sodium, mg	240		

Stir-fried Beef and Vegetables with Linguine

If you don't have linguine on hand, spaghetti works just as well.

6 ounces uncooked linguine, broken into 3-inch pieces

1 pound beef top round steak

1 teaspoon cornstarch

3/4 cup cold water

1/4 cup soy sauce

1 tablespoon cornstarch

1 tablespoon packed brown sugar

2 teaspoons white vinegar

1 teaspoon sesame oil

1/4 teaspoon pepper

1 tablespoon vegetable oil

2 teaspoons finely chopped gingerroot or 1 teaspoon ground ginger

1 tablespoon vegetable oil

2 cups bite-size pieces broccoli flowerets and stems

1 cup sliced mushrooms

1 red or yellow bell pepper, cut into bite-size strips

1/4 cup sliced green onions (2 to 3 medium)

Cook linguine as directed on package; drain. Meanwhile trim fat from beef steak. Cut beef with grain into 2-inch strips; cut strips across grain into 1/8-inch slices. (For ease in cutting, partially freeze beef about 1 1/2 hours.) Toss beef and 1 teaspoon cornstarch. Mix water, soy sauce, 1 tablespoon cornstarch, the brown sugar, vinegar, sesame oil and pepper.

Heat wok or 12-inch skillet until very hot. Add 1 tablespoon vegetable oil to wok; rotate wok to coat side. Add beef and gingerroot; stir-fry about 3 minutes or until beef is brown. Remove beef mixture from wok.

Add 1 tablespoon vegetable oil to wok; rotate wok to coat side. Add broccoli, mushrooms, bell pepper and onions; stir-fry about 4 minutes or until vegetables are crisp-tender. Stir in soy sauce mixture. Cook and stir about 1 minute or until thickened. Stir in beef mixture and linguine. Heat through. *4 servings.*

Nutrition Information Per Serving

1 serving		% of U.S. RDA	
Calories	455	Vitamin A	24%
Protein, g	35	Vitamin C	50%
Carbohydrate, g	50	Calcium	8%
Dietary fiber, g	5	Iron	32%
Fat, g	17		
Cholesterol, mg	65		
Sodium, mg	1280		

Sweet-and-Sour Lamb

This satisfying stir-fry is also delicious with beef or pork.

1 pound lamb boneless shoulder or leg

1 teaspoon cornstarch

4 medium stalks bok choy (with leaves)

⅓ cup red currant jelly

1 tablespoon cornstarch

3 tablespoons rice or white vinegar

3 tablespoons soy sauce

3 tablespoons water

1 teaspoon five-spice powder

1 tablespoon vegetable oil

2 cloves garlic, finely chopped

1 tablespoon vegetable oil

2 medium carrots, thinly sliced

1 medium green bell pepper, cut into ¾-inch pieces

1 medium onion, cut into thin wedges

Hot cooked brown rice

Trim fat from lamb. Cut lamb with grain into 2-inch strips; cut strips across grain into ⅛-inch slices. (For ease in cutting, partially freeze lamb about 1½ hours.) Toss lamb and 1 teaspoon cornstarch. Remove leaves from bok choy; cut leaves into ½-inch strips. Cut stems diagonally into ½-inch slices. Mix jelly, 1 tablespoon cornstarch, the vinegar, soy sauce, water and five-spice powder.

Heat wok or 12-inch skillet until very hot. Add 1 tablespoon oil to wok; rotate wok to coat side. Add lamb and garlic; stir-fry about 3 minutes or until lamb is brown. Remove from wok.

Add 1 tablespoon oil to wok; rotate wok to coat side. Add carrots; stir-fry 2 minutes. Add bok choy, bell pepper and onion; stir-fry about 3 minutes or until vegetables are crisp-tender. Stir in jelly mixture. Cook and stir about 1 minute or until thickened. Stir in lamb mixture. Heat through. Serve over rice. *4 servings.*

Nutrition Information Per Serving

1 serving		% of U.S. RDA	
Calories	495	Vitamin A	86%
Protein, g	37	Vitamin C	10%
Carbohydrate, g	50	Calcium	6%
Dietary fiber, g	4	Iron	22%
Fat, g	18		
Cholesterol, mg	100		
Sodium, mg	1170		

Cutting and Slicing for Stir-fry

When cutting meats and vegetables for stir-fries, start with a clean and very sharp knife or cleaver. Hold the food securely on the cutting surface with your fingertips. Your fingers should be curled so the knuckles almost touch the blade of the knife, acting as a guide as you move your hand back while cutting. For safety's sake, do not lift the cutting edge of the blade higher than the knuckles of the hand holding the food.

• To slice meat, place it in the freezer for about fifteen minutes or just until firm but not frozen. Cut the meat lengthwise, with the grain, into strips about two inches wide. Cut each strip across the grain into ⅛-inch strips.

• To slice celery and bok choy, cut straight across the stalk at the widest end. Cut across the stalk at an angle at the narrow end.

• To cut vegetables at an angle, keep the blade at an angle to the cutting surface while cutting.

Sweet Potato and Pork Stir-fry

1 pound pork boneless loin or leg

1 teaspoon cornstarch

1 tablespoon water

1 tablespoon cornstarch

1 tablespoon vegetable oil

2 cloves garlic, finely chopped

1 tablespoon vegetable oil

3 cups sliced mushrooms (about 8 ounces)

2 medium sweet potatoes or yams, cut lengthwise into fourths and thinly sliced

1 large onion, sliced

1/3 cup dry white wine or apple juice

1/3 cup cold water

1 teaspoon chicken bouillon granules

1/4 teaspoon crushed red pepper

Trim fat from pork. Cut pork with grain into 2-inch strips; cut strips across grain into 1/8-inch slices. (For ease in cutting, partially freeze pork about 1½ hours.) Toss pork and 1 teaspoon cornstarch. Mix 1 tablespoon water and 1 tablespoon cornstarch.

Heat wok or 12-inch skillet until very hot. Add 1 tablespoon oil to wok; rotate wok to coat side. Add pork and garlic; stir-fry about 3 minutes or until pork is brown. Remove pork mixture from wok.

Add 1 tablespoon oil to wok; rotate wok to coat side. Add mushrooms, sweet potatoes and onion; stir-fry 1 minute. Stir in wine, 1/3 cup water, bouillon granules and red pepper. Heat to boiling; reduce heat. Cover and simmer about 3 minutes or until potatoes are crisp-tender. Add cornstarch mixture. Cook and stir about 20 sec-

onds or until thickened. Stir in pork mixture. Heat through. Serve over hot cooked rice if desired. *4 servings.*

Nutrition Information Per Serving

1 serving		% of U.S. RDA	
Calories	325	Vitamin A	22%
Protein, g	36	Vitamin C	10%
Carbohydrate, g	20	Calcium	4%
Dietary fiber, g	4	Iron	24%
Fat, g	13		
Cholesterol, mg	110		
Sodium, mg	410		

Honeyed Chicken and Asparagus Stir-fry

(Photograph on page 33)

4 skinless boneless chicken breast halves (about 1 pound)

1 teaspoon cornstarch

1/3 cup chicken broth

1/4 cup dry white wine or chicken broth

1 tablespoon cornstarch

2 tablespoons soy sauce

2 tablespoons honey

1 teaspoon ground mustard

1/8 teaspoon pepper

1 tablespoon vegetable oil

1 tablespoon vegetable oil

2 cups 1-inch pieces asparagus (about 12 ounces)

2 medium tomatoes, cut into thin wedges

1 can (15 ounces) straw mushrooms, drained

Hot cooked brown rice

Cut chicken breast halves into bite-size pieces. Toss chicken and 1 teaspoon cornstarch. Mix broth, wine, 1 tablespoon cornstarch, the soy sauce, honey, mustard and pepper.

Heat wok or 12-inch skillet until very hot. Add 1 tablespoon oil to wok; rotate wok to coat side. Add chicken; stir-fry about 4 minutes or until chicken is white. Remove chicken from wok.

Add 1 tablespoon oil to wok; rotate wok to coat side. Add asparagus; stir-fry about 5 minutes or until asparagus is crisp-tender. Stir in broth mixture. Cook and stir about 1 minute or until thickened. Stir in chicken, tomatoes and mushrooms. Cook about 2 minutes or until heated through. Serve over rice. *4 servings.*

Nutrition Information Per Serving

1 serving		% of U.S. RDA	
Calories	400	Vitamin A	8%
Protein, g	34	Vitamin C	20%
Carbohydrate, g	44	Calcium	6%
Dietary fiber, g	5	Iron	18%
Fat, g	12		
Cholesterol, mg	65		
Sodium, mg	1370		

Timely Stir-fry Tips

When you stir-fry, you cook food in a small amount of oil. Ingredients are added in order of cooking time and stirred vigorously over high heat. The hot oil prevents sticking and seals in flavor and color, giving foods a shiny appearance. This quick method of cooking can be made even easier with these easy pre-planning tips.

• Vegetables and meat can be cut up and stored separately in the refrigerator for up to two days, or you can purchase pre-cut vegetables and meat from the supermarket. Keep in mind that uniformly cut, smaller and thinner pieces of food will cook more quickly. Seasonings and nonperishable sauce ingredients can be gathered, measured and organized several days ahead, too.

• If you plan to serve rice, it can be pre-cooked and reheated in the microwave. If you've forgotten about preparing regular rice, instant rice or couscous can be ready in five minutes!

• For best results, always start with a clean, dry wok and use vegetable or peanut oil as they tolerate high heat; margarine, butter and nonstick cooking sprays should not be used because they can burn. Heat wok over high heat before adding oil, then tilt it to coat the interior. To reduce the amount of fat in stir-fries, use a wok with a nonstick interior and instead of the 1 or more tablespoons of oil traditionally called for, reduce the amount to 1 or 2 teaspoons.

• Finally, assemble all your equipment and utensils before cooking and arrange all ingredients in the order in which they will be used. Read the recipe completely to make sure you understand each step and haven't forgotten anything.

Glazed Turkey and Pea Pods

Stir-fries make good use of turkey breast slices, which are easily cut into strips or pieces. A 6-ounce package of frozen Chinese pea pods, thawed, can be substituted for the fresh pea pods; stir them in with the turkey.

1 pound turkey breast slices

1 teaspoon cornstarch

¾ cup chicken broth

1 tablespoon cornstarch

3 tablespoons hoisin sauce

2 teaspoons chopped fresh gingerroot or 1 teaspoon ground ginger

⅛ teaspoon pepper

1 tablespoon vegetable oil

1 tablespoon vegetable oil

2 cups Chinese pea pods, strings removed

1 large red or green bell pepper, cut into ¾-inch pieces

2 cups frozen small whole onions, thawed

2 cups chow mein noodles

½ cup coarsely chopped cashews or peanuts

Cut turkey breast slices into bite-size pieces. Toss turkey and 1 teaspoon cornstarch. Mix broth, 1 tablespoon cornstarch, the hoisin sauce, gingerroot and pepper.

Heat wok or 12-inch skillet until very hot. Add 1 tablespoon oil to wok; rotate wok to coat side. Add turkey; stir-fry about 4 minutes or until turkey is white. Remove turkey from wok.

Add 1 tablespoon oil to wok; rotate wok to coat side. Add pea pods, bell pepper and onions; stir-fry 4 to 5 minutes or until vegetables are crisp-tender. Stir in hoisin sauce mixture. Cook and

stir about 1 minute or until thickened. Stir in turkey. Heat through. Stir in noodles and cashews. Serve immediately. *4 servings.*

Nutrition Information Per Serving

1 serving		% of U.S. RDA	
Calories	500	Vitamin A	12%
Protein, g	37	Vitamin C	30%
Carbohydrate, g	35	Calcium	8%
Dietary fiber, g	5	Iron	28%
Fat, g	26		
Cholesterol, mg	70		
Sodium, mg	820		

Stir-fried Tofu with Almonds

We used firm tofu instead of the soft variety, as it keeps its shape well when stir-fried.

4 ounces uncooked spinach fettuccine or regular fettuccine, broken into 3-inch pieces

½ cup beef broth

⅓ cup dry white wine or beef broth

1 tablespoon cornstarch

3 tablespoons hoisin sauce

⅛ teaspoon pepper

1 pound firm tofu, cut into ¾-inch cubes

1 tablespoon vegetable oil

1½ cups bite-size cauliflowerets

1 large red or green bell pepper, cut into bite-size strips

1 tablespoon vegetable oil

2 cloves garlic, finely chopped

⅓ cup sliced almonds, toasted

Cook fettuccine as directed on package; drain. Meanwhile, mix broth, wine, cornstarch, hoisin sauce and pepper. Drain tofu cubes thoroughly.

Heat wok or 12-inch skillet until very hot. Add 1 tablespoon oil to wok; rotate wok to coat side. Add cauliflowerets and bell pepper; stir-fry about 4 minutes or until vegetables are crisp-tender. Remove vegetables from wok.

Add 1 tablespoon oil to wok; rotate wok to coat side. Add tofu and garlic; gently stir-fry 5 minutes. Stir in broth mixture. Cook and stir about 1 minute or until thickened. Stir in vegetables and fettuccine. Heat through. Sprinkle with almonds. *4 servings.*

Nutrition Information Per Serving

1 serving		% of U.S. RDA	
Calories	430	Vitamin A	4%
Protein, g	26	Vitamin C	20%
Carbohydrate, g	33	Calcium	28%
Dietary fiber, g	6	Iron	80%
Fat, g	24		
Cholesterol, mg	25		
Sodium, mg	740		

Citrus Fish and Spinach Stir-fry

(Photograph on page 34)

4 ounces uncooked spaghetti, broken into 3-inch pieces

1 pound halibut, tuna, monkfish or swordfish steaks

½ cup orange juice

½ cup dry sherry or water

1 tablespoon cornstarch

1 tablespoon chopped fresh or 1 teaspoon dried basil leaves

1½ teaspoons chopped fresh or ½ teaspoon dried marjoram leaves

½ teaspoon salt

⅛ teaspoon pepper

1 tablespoon vegetable oil

3 medium carrots, thinly sliced (about 1½ cups)

1 large onion, sliced

1 tablespoon vegetable oil

4 cups bite-size pieces spinach

Cook spaghetti as directed on package; drain. Meanwhile, remove any skin and bones from fish. Cut fish into 1-inch pieces. Mix orange juice, sherry, cornstarch, basil, marjoram, salt and pepper.

Heat wok or 12-inch skillet until very hot. Add 1 tablespoon oil to wok; rotate wok to coat side. Add carrots and onion; stir-fry about 5 minutes or until vegetables are crisp-tender. Remove vegetables from wok.

Add 1 tablespoon oil to wok; rotate wok to coat side. Add fish; gently stir-fry about 4 minutes, trying to keep fish pieces intact, until fish flakes easily with fork. Carefully remove from wok.

Add orange juice mixture to wok. Cook and stir about 1 minute or until thickened. Stir in vegetables, fish, spaghetti and spinach. Cook about 1 minute or until mixture is heated through and spinach just starts to wilt. *4 servings.*

Nutrition Information Per Serving

1 serving		% of U.S. RDA	
Calories	350	Vitamin A	100%
Protein, g	30	Vitamin C	20%
Carbohydrate, g	42	Calcium	20%
Dietary fiber, g	5	Iron	20%
Fat, g	9		
Cholesterol, mg	60		
Sodium, mg	650		

Italian Mushroom Skillet

(Photograph on page 35)

Use any medium-size pasta, such as elbow macaroni, if you don't have shell macaroni.

1 pound ground beef

1 medium onion, chopped (about ½ cup)

2 cups sliced mushrooms

2 cloves garlic, finely chopped

1 jar (14 ounces) pizza sauce

1½ cups uncooked medium shell macaroni

1½ cups water

1 teaspoon sugar

1 teaspoon Italian seasoning

¾ cup shredded Italian-style four-cheese combination or Monterey Jack cheese (3 ounces)

Cook ground beef, onion, mushrooms and garlic in 12-inch skillet over medium heat, stirring frequently, until beef is brown and vegetables are tender; drain. Stir in pizza sauce, macaroni, water, sugar and Italian seasoning. Heat to boiling; reduce heat. Cover and simmer about 20 minutes, stirring frequently, until macaroni is tender.

Sprinkle with cheese. Cover and simmer 2 minutes or until cheese is melted. *4 servings.*

Nutrition Information Per Serving

1 serving		% of U.S. RDA	
Calories	565	Vitamin A	10%
Protein, g	34	Vitamin C	10%
Carbohydrate, g	54	Calcium	20%
Dietary fiber, g	5	Iron	32%
Fat, g	26		
Cholesterol, mg	80		
Sodium, mg	600		

Beef-Millet Pilaf

1 pound ground beef

2 large carrots, sliced (about 1½ cups)

1 large onion, chopped (about 1 cup)

2 medium stalks celery, sliced (about 1 cup)

1 cup uncooked millet*

3½ cups beef broth

1 tablespoon chopped fresh or 1 teaspoon dried thyme leaves

1½ teaspoons chopped fresh or ½ teaspoon dried sage leaves

Cook ground beef, carrots, onion and celery in 12-inch skillet over medium heat, stirring frequently, until beef is brown; drain. Stir in remaining ingredients. Heat to boiling; reduce heat. Cover and simmer about 25 minutes, stirring occasionally, until millet is tender. *4 servings.*

*1 cup uncooked regular brown rice can be substituted for the millet. Decrease beef broth to 2½ cups and increase simmer time to about 45 minutes or until brown rice is tender.

Nutrition Information Per Serving

1 serving		% of U.S. RDA	
Calories	385	Vitamin A	100%
Protein, g	28	Vitamin C	*
Carbohydrate, g	33	Calcium	6%
Dietary fiber, g	5	Iron	22%
Fat, g	18		
Cholesterol, mg	70		
Sodium, mg	690		

Sloppy Joe Skillet Dinner

1 pound lean ground beef

1½ cups whole kernel corn

1 medium onion, sliced and separated into rings

2 medium potatoes, thinly sliced

1 can (15½ ounces) sloppy joe sauce

Crumble ground beef into 10-inch skillet. Sprinkle corn over beef. Layer onion and potatoes on corn. Pour sloppy joe sauce over top. Cover and cook over low heat about 30 minutes or until beef is no longer pink and potatoes are tender. *4 servings.*

Nutrition Information Per Serving

1 serving		% of U.S. RDA	
Calories	420	Vitamin A	8%
Protein, g	25	Vitamin C	10%
Carbohydrate, g	39	Calcium	6%
Dietary fiber, g	6	Iron	22%
Fat, g	21		
Cholesterol, mg	65		
Sodium, mg	1000		

Corned Beef Hash

2 cups chopped cooked corned beef brisket*

2 cups whole kernel corn

1½ cups chopped cooked potatoes (about 1½ medium)

⅓ cup chopped onion

½ teaspoon salt

¼ teaspoon pepper

¼ cup shortening

Chopped fresh parsley

Mix all ingredients except shortening and parsley in large bowl. Heat shortening in 10-inch skillet over medium heat until melted. Spread beef mixture in skillet. Cook 10 to 15 minutes, turning occasionally with wide spatula, until brown. Sprinkle with parsley. *4 servings.*

*1 can (12 ounces) corned beef can be substituted for the brisket.

Nutrition Information Per Serving

1 serving		% of U.S. RDA	
Calories	405	Vitamin A	2%
Protein, g	16	Vitamin C	10%
Carbohydrate, g	31	Calcium	2%
Dietary fiber, g	4	Iron	12%
Fat, g	26		
Cholesterol, mg	70		
Sodium, mg	1080		

Veal Chow Mein

1 pound coarsely ground veal, beef or turkey

2 medium stalks celery, sliced (about 1 cup)

1 medium onion, sliced and separated into rings

2 cups bean sprouts (about 4 ounces)

¾ cup sliced mushrooms

1¼ cups beef broth

1 tablespoon soy sauce

¼ cup cold water

2 tablespoons cornstarch

3 cups chow mein noodles

Cook ground veal, celery and onion in 10-inch skillet over medium heat, stirring frequently, until veal is brown; drain. Stir in bean sprouts, mushrooms, broth and soy sauce.

Heat to boiling, stirring occasionally. Mix water and cornstarch; gradually stir into veal mixture.

Heat to boiling, stirring constantly. Boil and stir 1 minute. Serve over noodles. *4 servings.*

Nutrition Information Per Serving

1 serving		% of U.S. RDA	
Calories	330	Vitamin A	*
Protein, g	29	Vitamin C	6%
Carbohydrate, g	26	Calcium	6%
Dietary fiber, g	4	Iron	20%
Fat, g	14		
Cholesterol, mg	80		
Sodium, mg	650		

Lamb Fried Rice

1 tablespoon vegetable oil

½ pound lamb boneless loin or shoulder, cut into bite-size strips

1½ teaspoons finely chopped gingerroot or ¾ teaspoon ground ginger

1 tablespoon vegetable oil

1 cup chopped mushrooms

½ cup finely chopped bok choy (with leaves)

1 medium carrot, shredded (about ⅔ cup)

3 cups cold cooked rice

2 eggs, slightly beaten

3 tablespoons soy sauce

1 cup frozen green peas, thawed

Heat 1 tablespoon oil in 10-inch skillet over medium heat until hot. Cook lamb and gingerroot in oil, stirring frequently, until lamb is brown. Remove lamb mixture from skillet.

Add 1 tablespoon oil to skillet. Cook mushrooms, bok choy and carrot in oil 2 minutes, stirring frequently. Stir in rice. Cook about 2 minutes, stirring frequently and breaking up rice, until mixture is hot. Push rice mixture to side of skillet. Mix eggs and soy sauce in small bowl. Add egg mixture to skillet; cook and stir until eggs are thickened throughout but still moist. Stir egg mixture, peas and lamb mixture into rice mixture. Cook and stir until heated through. *4 servings.*

Nutrition Information Per Serving

1 serving		% of U.S. RDA	
Calories	495	Vitamin A	48%
Protein, g	24	Vitamin C	4%
Carbohydrate, g	53	Calcium	6%
Dietary fiber, g	4	Iron	28%
Fat, g	23		
Cholesterol, mg	160		
Sodium, mg	1730		

Lamb and Potato Skillet

(Photograph on page 36)

If you're fond of hash, you'll enjoy this tasty and colorful lamb version of the dish.

> *1 pound ground lamb*
> *1 medium leek, chopped*
> *1 clove garlic, finely chopped*
> *½ cup beef broth*
> *1 tablespoon chopped fresh or 1 teaspoon dried dill weed*
> *½ teaspoon salt*
> *¼ teaspoon pepper*
> *3 medium potatoes, quartered lengthwise and cut into ¼-inch pieces (about 3 cups)*
> *1 bay leaf*
> *2 small tomatoes, coarsely chopped (about 1 cup)*

Cook ground lamb, leek and garlic in 10-inch skillet over medium heat, stirring frequently, until lamb is brown; drain. Stir in remaining ingredients except tomatoes. Heat to boiling; reduce heat. Cover and simmer about 12 minutes, stirring occasionally, until potatoes are tender. Remove bay leaf. Stir in tomatoes. Heat through. *4 servings.*

Nutrition Information Per Serving

1 serving		% of U.S. RDA	
Calories	325	Vitamin A	18%
Protein, g	21	Vitamin C	20%
Carbohydrate, g	27	Calcium	4%
Dietary fiber, g	3	Iron	18%
Fat, g	16		
Cholesterol, mg	70		
Sodium, mg	410		

Pork and Peanut Skillet

(Photograph on page 36)

Walnuts or almonds instead of peanuts also work well in this curry-flavored dish.

> *1 tablespoon vegetable oil*
> *1 pound pork boneless loin or leg, cut into 1-inch pieces*
> *2 teaspoons curry powder*
> *1 cup shredded parsnips*
> *⅔ cup uncooked regular long grain rice*
> *¼ cup raisins*
> *2½ cups beef broth*
> *2 medium carrots, sliced (about 1 cup)*
> *¼ cup chopped fresh parsley*
> *¼ cup dry-roasted peanuts*

Heat oil in 10-inch skillet over medium heat until hot. Cook pork and curry powder in oil, stirring occasionally, until pork is brown. Stir in remaining ingredients except parsley and peanuts. Heat to boiling; reduce heat. Cover and simmer 30 minutes (do not lift cover or stir). Stir in parsley and peanuts, fluffing rice lightly with fork. *4 servings.*

Nutrition Information Per Serving

1 serving		% of U.S. RDA	
Calories	475	Vitamin A	82%
Protein, g	42	Vitamin C	10%
Carbohydrate, g	49	Calcium	6%
Dietary fiber, g	4	Iron	24%
Fat, g	14		
Cholesterol, mg	110		
Sodium, mg	550		

Pork Meatballs and Beans

(Photograph on page 37)

1 pound ground pork

½ cup dry bread crumbs

¼ cup apple juice

½ teaspoon ground mustard

¼ teaspoon salt

¼ teaspoon allspice

2 tablespoons vegetable oil

1 can (16 ounces) whole tomatoes, undrained

1 can (4 ounces) chopped green chiles, drained

1 small green bell pepper, chopped (about ½ cup)

1 medium onion, chopped (about ½ cup)

½ cup ketchup

1 can (15 to 16 ounces) great northern beans, rinsed and drained

1 can (15 to 16 ounces) garbanzo beans, rinsed and drained

Mix ground pork, bread crumbs, apple juice, mustard, salt and allspice. Shape mixture into forty 1-inch balls.

Heat 1 tablespoon of the oil in 10-inch skillet over medium-low heat until hot. Cook half of the meatballs in oil, stirring frequently, until brown; drain on paper towels. Repeat with remaining oil and meatballs. Return all meatballs to skillet.

Stir in tomatoes, chiles, bell pepper, onion and ketchup, breaking up tomatoes. Heat to boiling; reduce heat. Cover and simmer about 20 minutes, stirring occasionally, until meatballs are no longer pink in center. Stir in beans. Heat through. *4 servings.*

Nutrition Information Per Serving

1 serving		% of U.S. RDA	
Calories	660	Vitamin A	12%
Protein, g	38	Vitamin C	30%
Carbohydrate, g	68	Calcium	16%
Dietary fiber, g	11	Iron	42%
Fat, g	31		
Cholesterol, mg	70		
Sodium, mg	1410		

Ham and Hominy

1 small onion, chopped (about ¼ cup)

1 tablespoon margarine or butter

1 package (3 ounces) cream cheese, cut into cubes

¼ cup milk

2 cups cut-up fully cooked smoked ham

1 cup cooked green peas

1 can (16 ounces) hominy, drained

1 cup shredded spinach

Cook onion in margarine in 3-quart saucepan over medium heat about 5 minutes, stirring occasionally, until onion is tender. Stir in cream cheese and milk. Cook, stirring constantly, until cheese is melted. Stir in ham, peas and hominy. Cook, stirring occasionally, until hot; remove from heat. Stir in spinach until wilted. *4 servings.*

Nutrition Information Per Serving

1 serving		% of U.S. RDA	
Calories	385	Vitamin A	26%
Protein, g	21	Vitamin C	10%
Carbohydrate, g	30	Calcium	8%
Dietary fiber, g	6	Iron	18%
Fat, g	23		
Cholesterol, mg	70		
Sodium, mg	1110		

Polynesian Ham and Rice

1 can (20 ounces) pineapple chunks in juice, drained and juice reserved

1½ cups chicken broth

⅔ cup uncooked regular long grain rice

2 teaspoons curry powder

⅛ teaspoon ground red pepper (cayenne)

1 package (6 ounces) frozen Chinese pea pods, thawed

½ pound fully cooked smoked boneless ham, cut into ½-inch pieces

Mix reserved pineapple juice, the broth, rice, curry powder and red pepper in 10-inch skillet. Heat to boiling, stirring once or twice; reduce heat. Cover and simmer 20 minutes (do not lift cover or stir); remove from heat. Fluff rice lightly with fork. Cover and let steam 5 minutes.

Cut each pea pod crosswise in half. Stir pea pods, pineapple and ham into rice mixture. Cook over medium heat about 2 minutes, stirring once or twice, until mixture is heated through. *4 servings.*

Nutrition Information Per Serving

1 serving		% of U.S. RDA	
Calories	360	Vitamin A	2%
Protein, g	18	Vitamin C	30%
Carbohydrate, g	53	Calcium	6%
Dietary fiber, g	4	Iron	18%
Fat, g	10		
Cholesterol, mg	35		
Sodium, mg	830		

Spanish Chicken and Rice

This zesty main dish is perfect served with a simple lettuce salad topped with creamy cucumber dressing and warm tortillas.

1 tablespoon vegetable oil

4 skinless boneless chicken breast halves (about 1 pound)

⅔ cup uncooked regular brown rice

1½ cups chicken broth

1½ teaspoons chile powder

½ teaspoon sugar

½ teaspoon crushed red pepper

1 medium onion, chopped (about ½ cup)

2 cloves garlic, finely chopped

1 can (14½ ounces) stewed tomatoes

½ cup shredded Monterey Jack cheese (2 ounces)

Heat oil in 10-inch skillet over medium heat until hot. Cook chicken breast halves in oil, 8 to 10 minutes, turning once, until light brown. Drain fat from skillet. Stir remaining ingredients except cheese into skillet with chicken. Heat to boiling; reduce heat. Cover and simmer 50 to 55 minutes, stirring occasionally, until rice is tender. Sprinkle with cheese. *4 servings.*

Nutrition Information Per Serving

1 serving		% of U.S. RDA	
Calories	410	Vitamin A	18%
Protein, g	34	Vitamin C	20%
Carbohydrate, g	40	Calcium	16%
Dietary fiber, g	5	Iron	14%
Fat, g	15		
Cholesterol, mg	75		
Sodium, mg	710		

MOUTH-WATERING MUFFINS AND BISCUITS

Warm, fresh-from-the-oven muffins and biscuits are a lovely accompaniment to a one-dish dinner. Easy to mix and fast to bake, fresh muffins or biscuits make a meal extra-special, without a lot of extra work.

Oatmeal Muffins

1 egg

1 cup buttermilk

½ cup packed brown sugar

⅓ cup vegetable oil

1 cup quick-cooking oats

1 cup all-purpose flour

1 teaspoon baking powder

½ teaspoon salt

½ teaspoon baking soda

Heat oven to 400°. Grease bottoms only of 12 medium muffin cups, 2½ × 1¼ inches, or line with paper baking cups. Beat egg, buttermilk, brown sugar and oil in large bowl. Stir in remaining ingredients just until flour is moistened (batter will be lumpy). Divide batter evenly among muffin cups. Bake 20 to 25 minutes or until light brown. Immediately remove from pan. Serve warm. *1 dozen muffins.*

Nutrition Information Per Serving

1 muffin		% of U.S. RDA	
Calories	165	Vitamin A	*
Protein, g	3	Vitamin C	*
Carbohydrate, g	22	Calcium	6%
Dietary fiber, g	1	Iron	6%
Fat, g	7		
Cholesterol, mg	20		
Sodium, mg	190		

Relish Biscuits

(Photograph on page 39)

2 cups all-purpose flour

3 teaspoons baking powder

½ teaspoon salt

¼ cup vegetable oil

⅓ cup pickle relish, drained

¾ cup milk

Heat oven to 450°. Mix flour, baking powder and salt in large bowl. Stir in oil and relish. Stir in milk until dough leaves side of bowl (dough will be soft).

Turn dough onto lightly floured surface; gently roll in flour to coat. Knead lightly 10 times. Roll or pat ½ inch thick. Cut with floured 2-inch biscuit cutter. Place on ungreased cookie sheet about 1 inch apart for crusty sides, touching for soft sides. Bake 10 to 12 minutes or until golden brown. Immediately remove from cookie sheet. Serve hot. *About 1 dozen biscuits.*

Nutrition Information Per Serving

1 biscuit		% of U.S. RDA	
Calories	125	Vitamin A	*
Protein, g	2	Vitamin C	*
Carbohydrate, g	18	Calcium	8%
Dietary fiber, g	1	Iron	6%
Fat, g	5		
Cholesterol, mg	0		
Sodium, mg	240		

Chive Muffins

(Photograph on page 43)

1 egg

1 cup milk

¼ cup vegetable oil

1½ cups all-purpose flour

½ cup whole wheat flour

¼ cup sugar

¼ cup chopped fresh chives

3 teaspoons baking powder

½ teaspoon salt

Heat oven to 400°. Grease bottoms only of 12 medium muffin cups, 2½ × 1¼ inches, or line with paper baking cups. Beat egg, milk and oil in large bowl. Stir in remaining ingredients just until flour is moistened (batter will be lumpy). Divide batter among muffin cups. Bake 20 to 25 minutes or until golden brown. Immediately remove from pan. Serve warm. *1 dozen muffins.*

Nutrition Information Per Serving

1 muffin		% of U.S. RDA	
Calories	145	Vitamin A	*
Protein, g	3	Vitamin C	*
Carbohydrate, g	20	Calcium	8%
Dietary fiber, g	1	Iron	6%
Fat, g	6		
Cholesterol, mg	20		
Sodium, mg	200		

Cornmeal Biscuits

(Photograph on page 40)

½ cup (1 stick) firm margarine or butter

1½ cups all-purpose flour

½ cup yellow cornmeal

3 teaspoons baking powder

2 teaspoons sugar

½ teaspoon salt

¾ cup milk

Yellow cornmeal

Heat oven to 450°. Cut margarine into flour, ½ cup cornmeal, the baking powder, sugar and salt with pastry blender in large bowl until mixture resembles fine crumbs. Stir in milk until dough leaves side of bowl (dough will be soft).

Turn dough onto lightly floured surface; gently roll in flour to coat. Knead lightly 10 times. Roll or pat ½ inch thick. Cut with floured 2½-inch biscuit cutter. Place on ungreased cookie sheet about 1 inch apart for crusty sides, touching for soft sides. Sprinkle cornmeal lightly over biscuits. Bake 12 to 14 minutes or until golden brown. Immediately remove from cookie sheet. Serve hot. *About 1 dozen biscuits.*

Nutrition Information Per Serving

1 biscuit		% of U.S. RDA	
Calories	150	Vitamin A	10%
Protein, g	2	Vitamin C	*
Carbohydrate, g	18	Calcium	8%
Dietary fiber, g	1	Iron	6%
Fat, g	8		
Cholesterol, mg	0		
Sodium, mg	280		

Chicken-Vegetable Stroganoff

For a flavor twist try sour cream dip with onion or chives in place of the plain sour cream.

1½ cups frozen mixed broccoli, cauliflower and carrots

1½ cups sliced mushrooms

2 cups chicken broth

1 tablespoon chopped fresh or 1 teaspoon dried marjoram leaves

¼ teaspoon pepper

1 large onion, sliced

6 ounces uncooked egg noodles (3 to 3¾ cups)

2 cups cut-up cooked chicken

1 container (8 ounces) sour cream

⅓ cup water

2 tablespoons all-purpose flour

Heat mixed vegetables, mushrooms, broth, marjoram, pepper, onion and noodles to boiling in 10-inch skillet; reduce heat. Cover and simmer about 8 minutes, stirring occasionally, until noodles and vegetables are tender. Stir in chicken. Mix sour cream, water and flour; stir into chicken mixture. Heat to boiling. Boil and stir 1 minute. *4 servings.*

Nutrition Information Per Serving

1 serving		% of U.S. RDA	
Calories	440	Vitamin A	48%
Protein, g	33	Vitamin C	10%
Carbohydrate, g	43	Calcium	12%
Dietary fiber, g	6	Iron	28%
Fat, g	18		
Cholesterol, mg	130		
Sodium, mg	490		

Mexican Orzo Skillet

1 pound ground turkey

½ cup uncooked rosamarina (orzo) pasta

1 cup water

1 cup salsa

1 tablespoon chopped fresh cilantro or 1 teaspoon ground coriander

¼ teaspoon red pepper sauce

1 can (15 to 16 ounces) pinto beans, rinsed and drained

½ cup guacamole

Cook ground turkey in 10-inch skillet over medium heat, stirring frequently, until white; drain. Stir in remaining ingredients except guacamole. Heat to boiling; reduce heat. Cover and simmer about 15 minutes, stirring frequently, until pasta is tender. Serve with guacamole. *4 servings.*

Nutrition Information Per Serving

1 serving		% of U.S. RDA	
Calories	410	Vitamin A	12%
Protein, g	33	Vitamin C	10%
Carbohydrate, g	41	Calcium	8%
Dietary fiber, g	8	Iron	28%
Fat, g	16		
Cholesterol, mg	75		
Sodium, mg	1020		

Creamy Tuna Cavatelli

This tasty skillet dish also works well with canned salmon instead of tuna and shell macaroni in place of the cavatelli pasta.

2 cups uncooked cavatelli pasta (about 6 ounces)

1 package (10 ounces) frozen mixed vegetables

1½ cups water

1 bottle (8 ounces) clam juice

1 tablespoon chopped fresh or 1 teaspoon dried chervil leaves

¼ teaspoon pepper

2 tablespoons all-purpose flour

1 container (8 ounces) sour cream dip with chives

1 cup shredded process sharp American cheese (4 ounces)

1 can (9¼ ounces) tuna, drained and flaked

Heat cavatelli, vegetables, water, clam juice, chervil and pepper to boiling in 10-inch skillet; reduce heat. Cover and simmer 20 to 25 minutes, stirring occasionally, until cavatelli and vegetables are tender.

Stir flour into sour cream dip. Gradually stir sour cream dip, cheese and tuna into cavatelli mixture. Cook over medium heat, stirring occasionally, until hot. *4 servings*.

Nutrition Information Per Serving

1 serving		% of U.S. RDA	
Calories	510	Vitamin A	62%
Protein, g	35	Vitamin C	20%
Carbohydrate, g	40	Calcium	26%
Dietary fiber, g	4	Iron	22%
Fat, g	25		
Cholesterol, mg	110		
Sodium, mg	1250		

Clam-Artichoke Risotto

2 cans (6½ ounces each) minced clams, drained and liquid reserved

1 tablespoon margarine or butter

1 cup uncooked regular brown rice

1 large onion, chopped (about 1 cup)

1 large carrot, sliced (about ¾ cup)

1½ cups sliced mushrooms

¼ cup dry white wine or chicken broth

1 cup chicken broth

1 teaspoon Italian seasoning

1 jar (6 ounces) marinated artichoke hearts, drained

½ cup milk

¼ cup grated Parmesan cheese

Add enough water to reserved clam liquid to equal 1¼ cups; reserve. Heat margarine in 10-inch skillet over medium heat until melted. Stir in clams, rice, onion, carrot, mushrooms and wine. Cook about 4 minutes, stirring occasionally, or until wine is absorbed.

Stir in reserved clam liquid, broth and Italian seasoning. Heat to boiling; reduce heat. Cover and simmer 40 to 45 minutes, stirring occasionally, until rice is almost tender. Stir in artichoke hearts and milk. Heat through. Sprinkle with cheese. *4 servings*.

Nutrition Information Per Serving

1 serving		% of U.S. RDA	
Calories	430	Vitamin A	84%
Protein, g	35	Vitamin C	20%
Carbohydrate, g	57	Calcium	24%
Dietary fiber, g	7	Iron	100%
Fat, g	10		
Cholesterol, mg	70		
Sodium, mg	590		

Creamy Italian Shrimp

(Photograph on page 38)

*1 pound fresh or frozen raw medium
   shrimp (in shells)*

*6 ounces uncooked linguine or fettuccine,
   broken into 3-inch pieces*

1 tablespoon olive or vegetable oil

1 to 2 cloves garlic, finely chopped

1 tablespoon olive or vegetable oil

*2 small zucchini, cut lengthwise in half
   and thinly sliced (about 2 cups)*

1 cup half-and-half

¾ cup grated Parmesan cheese

¼ cup pesto

*1 tablespoon chopped fresh or 1 teaspoon
   dried rosemary leaves*

2 teaspoons lemon juice

¼ teaspoon pepper

*2 medium tomatoes, seeded and cut into
   bite-size pieces*

Peel shrimp. (If shrimp are frozen, do not thaw; peel in cold water.) Make a shallow cut lengthwise down back of each shrimp; wash out vein. Cook linguine as directed on package; drain. Rinse in cold water; drain.

Heat wok or 12-inch skillet until very hot. Add 1 tablespoon oil to wok; rotate wok to coat side. Add shrimp and garlic; stir-fry about 3 minutes or until shrimp are pink. Remove shrimp mixture from wok.

Add 1 tablespoon oil to wok; rotate wok to coat side. Add zucchini; stir-fry about 3 minutes or until crisp-tender. Stir in half-and-half, cheese, pesto, rosemary, lemon juice and pepper. Cook and stir 1 to 2 minutes or until slightly thickened. Stir in shrimp mixture, linguine and tomatoes. Cook about 1 minute or until heated through. *4 servings.*

Nutrition Information Per Serving

1 serving		% of U.S. RDA	
Calories	505	Vitamin A	16%
Protein, g	27	Vitamin C	10%
Carbohydrate, g	44	Calcium	34%
Dietary fiber, g	3	Iron	26%
Fat, g	26		
Cholesterol, mg	140		
Sodium, mg	700		

Greek Frittata

(Photograph on page 39)

No feta cheese on hand? Grated Parmesan cheese or shredded Cheddar cheese can be substituted for equally delicious results.

1 tablespoon vegetable oil

*1 cup frozen hash brown potatoes with
   onions and peppers*

*1 tablespoon chopped fresh or 1 teaspoon
   dried oregano leaves*

1½ cups bite-size pieces spinach

8 eggs

½ cup milk

¼ teaspoon salt

¼ teaspoon pepper

½ cup finely crumbled feta cheese

Heat oil in 10-inch ovenproof skillet over medium heat until hot. Cook potatoes and oregano in oil 3 minutes, stirring frequently. Stir in spinach. Cook about 1 minute, stirring frequently, until potatoes are tender and spinach starts to wilt. Reduce heat to medium-low.

Beat eggs, milk, salt and pepper in medium bowl until blended. Stir in cheese. Pour over potato mixture. Cover and cook 9 to 11 minutes or until eggs are set almost to center and are light brown on bottom.

Set oven control to broil. Broil frittata with top about 5 inches from heat about 2 minutes or until top just starts to brown. *4 servings.*

Nutrition Information Per Serving

1 serving		% of U.S. RDA	
Calories	315	Vitamin A	48%
Protein, g	17	Vitamin C	4%
Carbohydrate, g	13	Calcium	22%
Dietary fiber, g	1	Iron	14%
Fat, g	22		
Cholesterol, mg	440		
Sodium, mg	570		

◆─────────────────◆

Skillet Smarts

• Use a flat-bottomed pan of medium weight for even, quick heat and uniform cooking.

• With a gas cooking surface, adjust the flame to the pan size; with electric, fit the heating unit to the size of the pan.

• Use the lowest setting possible to achieve the desired cooking method. Turning the heat up and down can create hot spots and cause sticking.

• Always use the skillet size called for in a recipe. Not only does it affect the cooking time, it also affects the evaporation of liquids.

• Aluminum skillets are great heat conductors and easy to maintain. Stamped aluminum skillets are not as durable as cast aluminum, and unanodized aluminum pans can discolor certain foods.

• Stainless steel skillets are easy to maintain as they resist staining, pitting and corrosion but they do not conduct heat as well as aluminum. Aluminum-clad bottoms solve this problem.

◆─────────────────◆

Tortellini and Cheese

1 package (9 ounces) refrigerated or frozen cheese-filled tortellini

2 tablespoons margarine or butter

2 small zucchini, cut lengthwise in half and sliced ½ inch thick

1 large onion, chopped (about 1 cup)

2 tablespoons all-purpose flour

1 tablespoon chopped fresh or ¾ teaspoon dried dill weed

¼ teaspoon salt

¼ teaspoon pepper

1½ cups milk

1 cup shredded Swiss cheese (4 ounces)

Cook tortellini as directed on package; drain. Meanwhile heat margarine in 10-inch skillet over medium heat until melted. Cook zucchini and onion in margarine about 5 minutes, stirring frequently, until zucchini is crisp-tender.

Stir in flour, dill weed, salt and pepper. Cook over medium heat, stirring constantly, until bubbly; remove from heat. Stir in milk. Heat to boiling, stirring constantly. Boil and stir 1 minute. Stir in cheese until melted. Fold in tortellini. Heat through. *4 servings.*

Nutrition Information Per Serving

1 serving		% of U.S. RDA	
Calories	350	Vitamin A	22%
Protein, g	19	Vitamin C	*
Carbohydrate, g	25	Calcium	40%
Dietary fiber, g	2	Iron	10%
Fat, g	20		
Cholesterol, mg	110		
Sodium, mg	900		

Black-eyed Pea Medley

(Photograph on page 40)

If you like hot food, try adding a little extra hot pepper cheese.

4 slices bacon, cut into 1-inch pieces

2½ cups chicken broth

1 cup dried black-eyed peas, sorted and rinsed

2 medium stalks celery, sliced (about 1 cup)

1 large onion, chopped (about 1 cup)

1½ tablespoons chopped fresh or 1½ teaspoons dried savory leaves

1 clove garlic, finely chopped

3 medium carrots, thinly sliced (about 1½ cups)

1 large green bell pepper, cut into 1-inch pieces

½ cup shredded hot pepper cheese (2 ounces)

Cook bacon in 10-inch skillet over medium heat, stirring occasionally, until crisp. Remove bacon with slotted spoon and drain. Drain fat from skillet.

Heat broth, black-eyed peas, celery, onion, savory and garlic to boiling in same skillet. Boil uncovered 2 minutes; reduce heat. Cover and simmer about 40 minutes, stirring occasionally, until peas are almost tender. (Do not boil or peas will burst.) Stir in carrots and bell pepper. Heat to simmering. Cover and simmer about 13 minutes, stirring occasionally, until vegetables are tender; stir. Sprinkle with cheese and bacon. *4 servings.*

Nutrition Information Per Serving

1 serving		% of U.S. RDA	
Calories	255	Vitamin A	100%
Protein, g	19	Vitamin C	20%
Carbohydrate, g	36	Calcium	14%
Dietary fiber, g	14	Iron	26%
Fat, g	10		
Cholesterol, mg	20		
Sodium, mg	730		

Cooking with Cheese

Natural cheese is made from milk or cream from cows, sheep or goats; it is usually cured or aged to develop its flavor. Cheese can become tough and stringy if subjected to high heat or long cooking. Process cheese blends are made from natural cheese but have other added ingredients and are less susceptible to heat.

• To prevent cheese from becoming stringy, cook at low temperature and avoid overcooking. When adding cheese to hot foods, shred natural cheese and cube or slice process cheese for even, quick melting. Add it at the end of the preparation time and cook only until melted.

• Soft cheeses can be shredded or chopped more easily if they are first placed in the freezer for about fifteen minutes or just until firm but not frozen.

• To blend cheese easily, soften at room temperature.

STEWS, CHILES AND SOUPS

Italian Meatball Stew

1 pound ground beef

½ cup seasoned dry bread crumbs

⅓ cup finely chopped onion

¼ cup milk

¼ teaspoon salt

⅛ teaspoon pepper

1 egg

¾ cup water

1 teaspoon beef bouillon granules

½ teaspoon salt

⅛ teaspoon pepper

1 bay leaf

4 medium carrots, cut into 1-inch pieces

3 medium potatoes, cut into 1-inch cubes

2 medium stalks celery, cut into 1-inch pieces

1 can (14½ ounces) Italian-style stewed tomatoes

Mix ground beef, bread crumbs, onion, milk, ¼ teaspoon salt, ⅛ teaspoon pepper and the egg. Shape mixture by ¼ cupfuls into balls. Cook meatballs in Dutch oven over medium-high heat, stirring occasionally, until brown; drain fat from Dutch oven.

Stir in remaining ingredients. Heat to boiling; reduce heat. Cover and simmer about 40 minutes, stirring occasionally, until vegetables are tender. Remove bay leaf. *4 servings.*

Nutrition Information Per Serving

1 serving		% of U.S. RDA	
Calories	480	Vitamin A	100%
Protein, g	27	Vitamin C	20%
Carbohydrate, g	50	Calcium	10%
Dietary fiber, g	6	Iron	24%
Fat, g	22		
Cholesterol, mg	120		
Sodium, mg	1220		

Beef Stew with Thyme Dumplings

(Photograph on page 41)

1 tablespoon olive or vegetable oil

1½ pounds beef stew meat

4 cups water

1 teaspoon sugar

1 teaspoon lemon juice

1 teaspoon Worcestershire sauce

½ teaspoon salt

¼ teaspoon ground allspice

1 medium onion, sliced

1 small bay leaf

1 clove garlic, finely chopped

6 medium carrots, cut into fourths

3 medium potatoes, cut into eighths

3 medium parsnips, peeled and cut into fourths

½ cup cold water

2 tablespoons all-purpose flour

Thyme Dumplings (right)

Heat oil in Dutch oven over medium heat. Cook beef in oil, stirring occasionally, until light brown. Stir in 4 cups water, the sugar, lemon juice, Worcestershire sauce, salt, allspice, onion, bay leaf and garlic. Heat to boiling; reduce heat.

Cover and simmer 1 hour 45 minutes, adding water if necessary. Stir in carrots, potatoes and parsnips. Cover and simmer about 30 minutes or until beef and vegetables are tender.

Shake ½ cup cold water and the flour in tightly covered container; gradually stir into stew. Heat to boiling, stirring constantly. Boil and stir 1 minute; reduce heat.

Prepare Thyme Dumplings. Drop dumpling dough by 10 to 12 spoonfuls onto beef mixture (do not drop directly into liquid). Cook uncovered 10 minutes. Cover and cook 10 minutes longer. *6 servings.*

THYME DUMPLINGS

3 tablespoons shortening

1½ cups all-purpose flour

2 teaspoons baking powder

1½ teaspoons chopped fresh or ½ teaspoon dried thyme leaves

½ teaspoon salt

¾ cup milk

Cut shortening into remaining ingredients except milk with pastry blender in medium bowl until mixture resembles fine crumbs. Stir in milk just until blended.

Nutrition Information Per Serving

1 serving		% of U.S. RDA	
Calories	585	Vitamin A	100%
Protein, g	26	Vitamin C	10%
Carbohydrate, g	60	Calcium	18%
Dietary fiber, g	6	Iron	24%
Fat, g	30		
Cholesterol, mg	70		
Sodium, mg	610		

Hearty Veal Stew

1½ cups dried great northern beans, sorted and rinsed

3½ cups water

1 tablespoon vegetable oil

1 pound veal or beef stew meat

1 large onion, chopped (about 1 cup)

1 medium stalk celery (with leaves), sliced (about ½ cup)

1½ cups water

2 tablespoons chopped fresh or 2 teaspoons dried parsley leaves

1 tablespoon chopped fresh or 1 teaspoon dried basil leaves

1 teaspoon salt

¼ teaspoon pepper

3 small turnips, peeled and cubed (about 2 cups)

3 medium carrots, sliced (about 1½ cups)

¼ cup orange marmalade

5 roma (plum) tomatoes, chopped

Heat beans and 3½ cups water to boiling in Dutch oven. Boil uncovered 2 minutes; remove from heat. Cover and let stand 1 hour; drain.

Heat oven to 350°. Heat oil in ovenproof Dutch oven over medium-high heat. Cook veal, onion and celery in oil 6 to 8 minutes, stirring occasionally, until veal is brown and vegetables are crisp-tender. Stir in beans and remaining ingredients except marmalade and tomatoes. Heat to boiling; remove from heat. Cover and bake 1 hour. Stir in marmalade and tomatoes. Cover and bake 30 to 45 minutes longer or until veal and vegetables are tender. *6 servings.*

Nutrition Information Per Serving

1 serving		% of U.S. RDA	
Calories	350	Vitamin A	86%
Protein, g	32	Vitamin C	20%
Carbohydrate, g	48	Calcium	16%
Dietary fiber, g	10	Iron	32%
Fat, g	8		
Cholesterol, mg	80		
Sodium, mg	490		

Edible Bowls

Edible bowls are a fun and tasty way to serve up stew, chile or soup! Pick one of our bowls or come up with one of your own. Be sure to place edible bowls on dinner plates or in soup bowls before filling.

• Snazzy Pepper Bowls—Cut thin slice from stem end of peppers; remove seeds and membranes. Fill bell peppers just before serving; replace tops.

• Crunchy Cabbage Bowls—Cut heads of cabbage in half and cut out the inner cabbage leaves, leaving a one-inch-thick wall to form the bowl.

• Sunny Squash Bowls—Cut round winter squash, such as acorn or buttercup, lengthwise in half; remove seeds and fibers. Cook squash as desired before filling or use uncooked.

• Chewy Bread Bowls—Cut off tops of small, round bread loaves and scoop out the bread, leaving a one-inch-thick wall. Fill loaves; replace tops.

• Crispy Tortilla Bowls—Brush both sides of tortillas with melted margarine. Place each tortilla in ovenproof bowl, making pleats as needed to fit. Bake tortillas in bowls in 400° oven for ten to fifteen minutes or until crisp and golden brown. Cool tortillas in bowls.

Curried Lentil Stew

Browned in a little oil before being cooked in liquid, the lentils retain their shape instead of becoming mushy.

2 to 3 tablespoons olive or vegetable oil

2 skinless boneless chicken breast halves (½ to ¾ pound)

1½ cups dried lentils, sorted and rinsed

½ cup chopped red onion

1 red bell pepper, cut into ½-inch squares

3 cloves garlic, finely chopped

½ cup uncooked regular long grain rice

2½ cups water

2 cups chicken broth

2 teaspoons curry powder

1 teaspoon ground coriander

½ teaspoon ground ginger

½ teaspoon red pepper sauce

½ cup plain yogurt

Heat 1 tablespoon of the oil in Dutch oven over medium heat. Cook chicken breast halves in oil 8 to 10 minutes, turning once, until light brown. Add lentils, onion, bell pepper and garlic. Cook 3 to 5 minutes, stirring occasionally, until onion is crisp-tender and lentils are slightly browned, adding remaining oil if necessary. Stir in remaining ingredients except yogurt. Heat to boiling; reduce heat. Cover and simmer about 20 minutes or until lentils and rice are tender and juices of chicken run clear. Top each serving with yogurt. *4 servings.*

Nutrition Information Per Serving

1 serving		% of U.S. RDA	
Calories	480	Vitamin A	8%
Protein, g	38	Vitamin C	30%
Carbohydrate, g	76	Calcium	14%
Dietary fiber, g	13	Iron	50%
Fat, g	11		
Cholesterol, mg	35		
Sodium, mg	450		

Pumpkin-Chicken Stew

(Photograph on page 42)

If you don't have pumpkin pie spice, you can use ½ teaspoon ground cinnamon, ¼ teaspoon ground ginger and ⅛ teaspoon each ground nutmeg and ground allspice.

¼ cup all-purpose flour

½ teaspoon salt

¼ teaspoon paprika

¼ teaspoon pepper

4 skinless boneless chicken breast halves (about 1 pound), cut into 1-inch pieces

1 tablespoon vegetable oil

2½ cups 1-inch cubes pumpkin or Hubbard squash

2 cups chicken broth

1 teaspoon pumpkin pie spice

3 medium potatoes, cut into 1-inch cubes

1 medium onion, chopped (about ½ cup)

1 clove garlic, finely chopped

1 can (16 ounces) stewed tomatoes

Mix flour, salt, paprika and pepper. Coat chicken with flour mixture. Heat oil in Dutch oven over medium heat. Cook chicken in oil 8 to 10 minutes, stirring occasionally, until white.

Stir in remaining ingredients. Heat to boiling; reduce heat. Cover and simmer about 30 minutes or until vegetables are tender. Sprinkle with chopped parsley if desired. *4 servings.*

Nutrition Information Per Serving

1 serving		% of U.S. RDA	
Calories	390	Vitamin A	100%
Protein, g	32	Vitamin C	30%
Carbohydrate, g	46	Calcium	6%
Dietary fiber, g	5	Iron	22%
Fat, g	11		
Cholesterol, mg	60		
Sodium, mg	1000		

Seafood-Rice Stew

(Photograph on page 43)

1 tablespoon margarine or butter

1 medium onion, sliced

4 cups chicken broth

2 medium carrots, cut into ¼-inch slices (about 1 cup)

½ cup uncooked regular long grain rice

1 tablespoon lemon juice

1 teaspoon chopped fresh or ¼ teaspoon dried dill weed

1 teaspoon chopped fresh or ¼ teaspoon dried thyme leaves

½ teaspoon salt

⅛ teaspoon pepper

1 package (16 ounces) frozen sugar snap peas, thawed

1 pound sole or other lean fish fillets, cut into 1-inch pieces

1 package (6 ounces) frozen cooked tiny shrimp, thawed

1 cup sliced mushrooms (about 3 ounces)

Heat margarine in Dutch oven over medium heat. Cook onion in margarine about 5 minutes, stirring occasionally, until tender. Stir in broth, carrots, rice, lemon juice, dill weed, thyme, salt and pepper. Heat to boiling; reduce heat. Cover and simmer about 20 minutes or until rice is tender.

Stir peas into rice mixture. Heat to boiling; reduce heat. Cover and simmer 5 minutes. Stir in fish, shrimp and mushrooms. Cover and simmer 5 to 8 minutes or until fish flakes easily with fork. *6 servings.*

Nutrition Information Per Serving

1 serving		% of U.S. RDA	
Calories	235	Vitamin A	62%
Protein, g	26	Vitamin C	4%
Carbohydrate, g	29	Calcium	6%
Dietary fiber, g	5	Iron	18%
Fat, g	4		
Cholesterol, mg	75		
Sodium, mg	890		

Ravioli and Eggplant Stew

3 tablespoons olive or vegetable oil

2 cups cubed peeled eggplant

1 can (14½ ounces) Italian-style stewed tomatoes

1½ teaspoons chopped fresh or ½ teaspoon dried basil leaves

1 cup water

2 small zucchini, cut lengthwise in half and sliced ½ inch thick (about 2 cups)

1 package (9 ounces) refrigerated cheese-filled ravioli

1 cup freshly grated Parmesan cheese (about 3 ounces)

Heat oil in large 12-inch skillet over medium-high heat. Cook eggplant in oil 5 minutes, stirring occasionally. Stir in tomatoes and basil. Heat to boiling; reduce heat. Cover and simmer about 15 minutes, stirring once or twice, until eggplant is tender. Stir in water, zucchini and ravioli. Heat to boiling; reduce heat. Cover and simmer 10 minutes, stirring once or twice, until ravioli are tender. Sprinkle with cheese. Cover and heat about 5 minutes or until cheese is melted. *4 servings.*

Nutrition Information Per Serving

1 serving		% of U.S. RDA	
Calories	405	Vitamin A	18%
Protein, g	20	Vitamin C	10%
Carbohydrate, g	32	Calcium	50%
Dietary fiber, g	5	Iron	16%
Fat, g	24		
Cholesterol, mg	110		
Sodium, mg	700		

Garbanzo-Chutney Stew

The sweet chutney and apple juice complement the beans and squash in this delightful, Indian-inspired meatless meal.

1 package (16 ounces) dried garbanzo beans, sorted and rinsed

8 cups water

2 tablespoons olive or vegetable oil

1 large onion, sliced

½ cup chutney

2 cups water

2 cups apple juice

2 teaspoons curry powder

1 teaspoon salt

1 small butternut squash (about 1½ pounds), peeled and cubed

2 large tomatoes, chopped (about 2 cups)

2 tablespoons chopped fresh cilantro, if desired

4 cups hot cooked couscous or rice

Heat beans and 8 cups water to boiling in Dutch oven. Boil 2 minutes; remove from heat. Cover and let stand 1 hour; drain.

Heat oil in Dutch oven over medium-high heat. Cook onion in oil about 5 minutes, stirring occasionally, until tender. Stir in beans, chutney, 2 cups water, the apple juice and curry powder. Heat to boiling; reduce heat. Cover and simmer 2½ to 3 hours or until beans are tender.

Stir in salt and squash. Cover and simmer about 20 minutes or until squash is tender. Stir in tomatoes and cilantro; heat through. Serve over couscous and, if desired, with additional chutney and shredded coconut. *8 servings.*

Nutrition Information Per Serving

1 serving		% of U.S. RDA	
Calories	365	Vitamin A	30%
Protein, g	14	Vitamin C	10%
Carbohydrate, g	73	Calcium	8%
Dietary fiber, g	11	Iron	26%
Fat, g	7		
Cholesterol, mg	0		
Sodium, mg	290		

Nutrition Information Per Serving

1 serving		% of U.S. RDA	
Calories	400	Vitamin A	14%
Protein, g	29	Vitamin C	10%
Carbohydrate, g	35	Calcium	10%
Dietary fiber, g	11	Iron	36%
Fat, g	21		
Cholesterol, mg	65		
Sodium, mg	520		

Chile con Carne

1 pound beef boneless chuck, tip or round steak, cut into 1-inch squares

1 large onion, chopped (about 1 cup)

2 cloves garlic, crushed

1 tablespoon chile powder

1 teaspoon ground cumin

1 teaspoon dried oregano leaves

1 teaspoon cocoa

¼ teaspoon red pepper sauce

1 can (16 ounces) whole tomatoes, undrained

1 can (15 to 16 ounces) dark kidney beans, undrained

Cook beef, onion and garlic in 3-quart saucepan over medium heat, stirring occasionally, until beef is brown; drain. Stir in remaining ingredients except beans, breaking up tomatoes. Heat to boiling; reduce heat. Cover and simmer about 1 hour, stirring occasionally, until beef is tender.

Stir in beans. Heat to boiling; reduce heat. Simmer uncovered about 20 minutes, stirring occasionally, until desired thickness. *4 servings.*

Chile Madness

Tired of sour cream, chopped onion or shredded cheese on your chile? Here are some ideas that truly are tops!

• Top each serving with a crunchy snack mix featuring cereals or miniature crackers.

• Sprinkle broken tortilla chips and shredded cheese on top of individual servings in microwavable bowls. Zap them in the microwave just until the cheese is melted.

• Make your own tortilla toppers: Brush flour tortillas with melted margarine and sprinkle with pepper. Cut into desired shapes and bake on an ungreased cookie sheet at 400° for 8 to 10 minutes or until golden brown.

• Use sturdy restaurant-style tortilla chips as scoops to eat with instead of spoons.

German Sauerkraut Stew

While spaetzle adds a fun and authentic touch to this flavorful dish, small shell pasta also can be used. If you'd like to reduce the sodium here, rinse and drain the sauerkraut.

4 slices bacon

1 pound pork boneless ribs or shoulder, cubed

½ cup chopped red onion

1 can (16 ounces) sauerkraut, drained

1½ cups dry white wine or chicken broth

2½ cups water

1 medium apple, peeled and diced

1 teaspoon juniper berries, if desired

½ teaspoon pepper

2 bay leaves

4 small new potatoes, cut into fourths

2 medium carrots, diced (about 1 cup)

1 cup uncooked dried spaetzle

Sour cream, if desired

Heat oven to 325°. Cook bacon in ovenproof Dutch oven over medium-high heat until crisp. Drain bacon, reserving 1 tablespoon fat in Dutch oven. Crumble bacon and reserve. Cook pork and onion in fat over medium heat 5 to 8 minutes, stirring occasionally, until pork is no longer pink. Stir in sauerkraut, wine, water, apple, juniper berries, pepper and bay leaves. Heat to boiling; remove from heat. Cover and bake 1 hour.

Stir in potatoes and carrots. Cover and bake 45 to 50 minutes or until pork and vegetables are tender. Stir in spaetzle. Cover and bake 12 to 15 minutes, stirring and pushing spaetzle down into broth once or twice, until spaetzle is tender. Remove bay leaves. Top each serving with sour cream and bacon. *5 servings.*

Nutrition Information Per Serving

1 serving		% of U.S. RDA	
Calories	425	Vitamin A	66%
Protein, g	20	Vitamin C	10%
Carbohydrate, g	44	Calcium	8%
Dietary fiber, g	7	Iron	20%
Fat, g	22		
Cholesterol, mg	100		
Sodium, mg	870		

▲ *Honeyed Chicken and Asparagus Stir-fry* (Recipe on page 8)

▲ *Italian Mushroom Skillet* (Recipe on page 12)

◄ *Citrus Fish and Spinach Stir-fry* (Recipe on page 11)

▲ *Pork Meatballs and Beans* (Recipe on page 16)

◄ *Lamb and Potato Skillet* (Recipe on page 15); *Pork and Peanut Skillet*
(Recipe on page 15)

37

▲ *Greek Frittata* (Recipe on page 22); *Relish Biscuits* (Recipe on page 18)

◄ *Creamy Italian Shrimp* (Recipe on page 22); *Italian Bread with Herb Spread* (Recipe on page 119)

▲ *Beef Stew with Thyme Dumplings* (Recipe on page 26)

◄ *Black-eyed Pea Medley* (Recipe on page 24); *Cornmeal Biscuits* (Recipe on page 19)

▲ *Seafood-Rice Stew* (Recipe on page 29); *Chive Muffins* (Recipe on page 19)

◄ *Golden Peanut Chicken Soup* (Recipe on page 64); *Pumpkin-Chicken Stew* (Recipe on page 28)

▲ *Chile Verde with Fresh Tomato Salsa* (Recipe on page 52)

◄ *Smoky Bacon and Three-Bean Chile* (Recipe on page 52)

▲ *Scandinavian Split Pea and Barley Soup* (Recipe on page 56);
Chicken-Tortellini Soup (Recipe on page 58)

◄ *Borsch* (Recipe on page 54)

Wild Rice Chowder (Recipe on page 63) ►

Chicken and Cornmeal Dumpling Stew

This rustic stew uses a whole cut-up chicken. To make chicken a bit more manageable, cut each half chicken breast in half again.

1 tablespoon vegetable oil

2¹/₂- to 3-pound cut-up broiler-fryer chicken

1 large onion, chopped (about 1 cup)

2 cloves garlic, finely chopped

1 jalapeño chile, seeded and finely chopped

1 cup pitted ripe olives, cut in half

1 cup frozen corn with red and green peppers, thawed

2 teaspoons chile powder

2 teaspoons ground cumin

1 can (28 ounces) Italian pear-shaped tomatoes, undrained

Cornmeal Dumplings (right)

Heat oil in Dutch oven over medium heat. Cook chicken in oil 10 to 12 minutes or until golden brown on all sides. Remove chicken from Dutch oven. Drain all but 1 tablespoon fat from Dutch oven. Cook onion, garlic and chile in fat 2 to 3 minutes, stirring occasionally, until onion is crisp-tender. Add chicken and remaining ingredients except Cornmeal Dumplings, breaking up tomatoes. Heat to boiling; reduce heat. Cover and simmer 20 minutes.

Prepare Cornmeal Dumplings; drop dough by spoonfuls onto chicken mixture (do not drop directly into liquid). Cover and simmer 20 minutes or until juices of thickest pieces of chicken run clear. *6 servings*.

CORNMEAL DUMPLINGS

¹/₂ cup all-purpose flour

¹/₂ cup yellow cornmeal

¹/₄ cup milk

2 tablespoons vegetable oil

1 teaspoon baking powder

¹/₂ teaspoon salt

¹/₄ teaspoon ground thyme

1 egg

1 small onion, finely chopped (about ¹/₄ cup)

Mix all ingredients.

CHICKEN TAMALE STEW: Omit Cornmeal Dumplings. Increase first simmer time to 40 minutes. Carefully unwrap tamales from 1 can (14³/₄ ounces) tamales with chile sauce. Cut crosswise in half. Place on stew. Cover and cook about 5 minutes or until thoroughly heated.

Nutrition Information Per Serving

1 serving		% of U.S. RDA	
Calories	335	Vitamin A	22%
Protein, g	28	Vitamin C	30%
Carbohydrate, g	34	Calcium	14%
Dietary fiber, g	5	Iron	24%
Fat, g	12		
Cholesterol, mg	100		
Sodium, mg	1150		

Baked Lima Bean Chile

With this chile, you mix the ingredients, put it in the oven and then go about your business. This hearty chile bakes while you garden, shop, study or enjoy family and friends. If you don't have an ovenproof Dutch oven, cover the handles of your regular Dutch oven with foil.

1½ cups dried lima beans, sorted and rinsed

6 cups water

2 tablespoons chile powder

1 teaspoon cumin seed

1 teaspoon salt

¼ teaspoon ground red pepper (cayenne)

1 pound beef boneless chuck, tip or round steak, cut into 1-inch pieces

3 medium onions, chopped (about 1½ cups)

3 cloves garlic, finely chopped

3 cans (8 ounces each) tomato sauce

Heat oven to 325°. Heat beans and water to boiling in ovenproof Dutch oven. Boil 2 minutes. Stir in remaining ingredients; remove from heat. Cover and bake about 4 hours or until beef and beans are tender; stir. Top each serving with sour cream, chopped onion and shredded Cheddar cheese if desired. *6 servings.*

Nutrition Information Per Serving

1 serving		% of U.S. RDA	
Calories	335	Vitamin A	20%
Protein, g	23	Vitamin C	10%
Carbohydrate, g	38	Calcium	6%
Dietary fiber, g	11	Iron	30%
Fat, g	15		
Cholesterol, mg	45		
Sodium, mg	1100		

Cooking With Dried Beans

The variety of beans, peas and lentils—known as legumes—make them a welcome addition to many types of dishes. They can be used to extend the protein of meats, cheeses and eggs, or be combined with grains, such as corn, wheat and rice, to form a complete protein. They are packed with fiber as well as flavor.

• Except for lentils, dried beans need to be boiled, uncovered, for two minutes before cooking to destroy an enzyme that can cause some people to become sick. Except for the initial boiling, they should be simmered and not boiled during the remaining cooking time so the skins will not burst.

• Although not necessary, soaking allows for more uniform swelling. Drain soaking water and replace with fresh liquid before cooking. Add 1 tablespoon of margarine or vegetable oil to the cooking water of beans to prevent foaming. Drain and rinse after cooking.

• Add salt and acidic foods, such as lemon juice, vinegar, tomatoes and tomato sauce, paste or juice, after the beans are soft as they tend to toughen beans. Dried beans triple in volume during cooking and can be interchanged in recipes with similar size beans.

• Beans are done when they can be pierced all the way through with a fork or the tip of a knife. Store cooked beans covered up to four days in the refrigerator or up to three months in the freezer.

• Canned beans can be substituted for many dried beans when cooking, but the liquid amounts and cooking times need to be adjusted. Canned beans need only be heated and should be added during the last ten minutes of cooking time.

Fiesta Pork Chile

1 large onion, chopped (about 1 cup)

2 medium green bell peppers, chopped (about 2 cups)

2 cloves garlic, finely chopped

1 pound ground pork

2 cups salsa

2 teaspoons chile powder

2 cans (15 to 16 ounces each) pinto beans, rinsed and drained

2 cans (16 ounces each) whole tomatoes, undrained

1 package (16 ounces) frozen corn with red and green peppers

Cook onion, bell peppers, garlic and ground pork in Dutch oven over medium heat, stirring frequently, until pork is no longer pink; drain if necessary. Stir in remaining ingredients, breaking up tomatoes. Heat to boiling; reduce heat. Cover and simmer 10 minutes. *6 servings.*

Nutrition Information Per Serving

1 serving		% of U.S. RDA	
Calories	435	Vitamin A	20%
Protein, g	27	Vitamin C	30%
Carbohydrate, g	59	Calcium	12%
Dietary fiber, g	13	Iron	30%
Fat, g	16		
Cholesterol, mg	45		
Sodium, mg	1540		

Turkey Chile Mole

1 pound ground turkey

1 small onion, chopped (about ¼ cup)

¼ cup chopped green bell pepper

2 jalapeño chiles, seeded and finely chopped

1 clove garlic, finely chopped

1 tablespoon plum or grape preserves

2 teaspoons chile powder

1 teaspoon ground cumin

½ teaspoon salt

¼ teaspoon pepper

1 ounce unsweetened chocolate, chopped

1 can (28 ounces) Italian pear-shaped tomatoes, undrained

1 can (15 to 16 ounces) kidney beans, rinsed and drained

Cook ground turkey, onion, bell pepper, chiles and garlic in Dutch oven over medium heat 5 to 8 minutes, stirring occasionally, until turkey is done. Stir in remaining ingredients, breaking up tomatoes. Heat to boiling; reduce heat. Cover and simmer 30 minutes. *4 servings.*

Nutrition Information Per Serving

1 serving		% of U.S. RDA	
Calories	400	Vitamin A	40%
Protein, g	33	Vitamin C	50%
Carbohydrate, g	37	Calcium	12%
Dietary fiber, g	11	Iron	36%
Fat, g	17		
Cholesterol, mg	75		
Sodium, mg	870		

Chile Verde with Fresh Tomato Salsa

(Photograph on page 45)

2 cups chopped cooked chicken breast

1½ cups chicken broth

1 can (15 to 16 ounces) cannellini or great northern beans, rinsed and drained

1 package (9 ounces) frozen shoepeg white or regular whole kernel corn, thawed

1 can (7 ounces) salsa verde or ¾ cup green taco sauce

¼ cup chopped fresh cilantro

Fresh Tomato Salsa (below)

Mix all ingredients except cilantro and Fresh Tomato Salsa in 3-quart saucepan. Heat to boiling; reduce heat. Cover and simmer 20 minutes. Stir in cilantro. Serve with Fresh Tomato Salsa. *4 servings.*

FRESH TOMATO SALSA

¼ cup sliced green onions (2 to 3 medium)

¼ teaspoon grated lime peel

2 tablespoons lime juice

1 large tomato, chopped (about 1 cup)

1 jalapeño chile, seeded and finely chopped

Mix all ingredients thoroughly.

Nutrition Information Per Serving

1 serving		% of U.S. RDA	
Calories	305	Vitamin A	20%
Protein, g	34	Vitamin C	40%
Carbohydrate, g	41	Calcium	10%
Dietary fiber, g	8	Iron	28%
Fat, g	4		
Cholesterol, mg	55		
Sodium, mg	1060		

Smoky Bacon and Three-Bean Chile

(Photograph on page 44)

Chipotle chiles are smoked, dried jalapeños. They are brown and wrinkled, and must be soaked before use. They add a wonderful smoky flavor that cannot be duplicated. For spicier chile, use another dried chile or two.

¼ cup sun-dried tomato halves (not oil-packed)

2 dried chipotle chiles

1 cup boiling water

2 slices bacon, diced

1 large onion, chopped (about 1 cup)

½ pound Canadian-style bacon, cubed

1 yellow bell pepper, cut into 1-inch squares

1 red bell pepper, cut into 1-inch squares

1 can (15 to 16 ounces) dark red kidney beans, rinsed and drained

1 can (15 ounces) black beans, rinsed and drained

1 can (15 to 16 ounces) black-eyed peas, undrained

Soak tomatoes and chiles in boiling water 10 minutes; drain, reserving water. Chop tomatoes and chiles.

Cook bacon in Dutch oven until crisp. Push bacon to side of Dutch oven. Cook onion, Canadian-style bacon and bell peppers in bacon fat over medium-high heat about 3 minutes, stirring occasionally, until vegetables are crisp-tender. Stir in tomatoes, chiles, reserved water and remaining ingredients. Heat to boiling; reduce heat. Cover and simmer 20 minutes. *4 servings.*

Nutrition Information Per Serving

1 serving		% of U.S. RDA	
Calories	370	Vitamin A	30%
Protein, g	33	Vitamin C	50%
Carbohydrate, g	65	Calcium	12%
Dietary fiber, g	21	Iron	40%
Fat, g	7		
Cholesterol, mg	30		
Sodium, mg	1340		

Wild Rice Burgundy Soup

1 tablespoon margarine or butter

³/₄ pound beef sirloin steak, cut into ¹/₂-inch pieces

4 medium carrots, sliced (about 2 cups)

1 medium onion, chopped (about ¹/₂ cup)

1 small stalk celery, diced (about ¹/₄ cup)

³/₄ cup uncooked wild rice

3 cups beef broth

1 cup red Burgundy, other dry red wine or beef broth

1 tablespoon chopped fresh or 1 teaspoon dried thyme leaves

¹/₂ teaspoon salt

¹/₄ teaspoon pepper

2 tablespoons all-purpose flour

¹/₄ cup water

Heat margarine in Dutch oven over medium heat until melted. Cook beef in margarine, stirring occasionally, until brown. Remove beef from Dutch oven. Cook carrots, onion and celery in Dutch oven about 3 minutes, stirring occasionally, until onion is crisp-tender (add 1 tablespoon margarine if necessary). Stir in beef and remaining ingredients except flour and water. Heat to boiling; reduce heat. Cover and simmer 30 to 35 minutes or until rice and beef are tender. Mix flour and water; stir into soup. Heat to boiling; boil 1 minute, stirring frequently. *4 servings.*

Nutrition Information Per Serving

1 serving		% of U.S. RDA	
Calories	370	Vitamin A	100%
Protein, g	26	Vitamin C	*
Carbohydrate, g	41	Calcium	6%
Dietary fiber, g	4	Iron	24%
Fat, g	13		
Cholesterol, mg	50		
Sodium, mg	880		

Borsch

(Photograph on page 46)

½ cup dried navy beans, sorted and rinsed

6 cups water

1 pound beef boneless chuck, tip or round steak, cut into ½-inch cubes

1 smoked pork hock

1 teaspoon salt

¼ teaspoon pepper

1 can (10½ ounces) condensed beef broth

3 cups shredded cabbage

6 medium beets, shredded

2 medium potatoes, cut into cubes (about 2 cups)

2 medium onions, sliced

2 cloves garlic, chopped

2 teaspoons dill seed or 1 sprig dill weed

1 tablespoon pickling spice

¼ cup red wine vinegar

½ cup sour cream

Heat beans and water to boiling in Dutch oven. Boil 2 minutes; remove from heat. Cover and let stand 1 hour.

Add beef, pork, salt, pepper and broth to beans. Heat to boiling; reduce heat. Cover and simmer 1 to 1½ hours or until beef is tender.

Remove pork from Dutch oven; cool pork about 10 minutes or just until cool enough to handle. Remove pork from bone; cut pork into bite-size pieces. Stir pork, cabbage, beets, potatoes, onions and garlic into soup. Tie dill seed and pickling spice in cheesecloth bag, or place in tea ball, and add to soup. Cover and simmer 2 hours.

Stir in vinegar. Simmer 10 minutes. Remove cheesecloth bag. Serve sour cream with soup. Sprinkle with chopped fresh dill weed if desired. *6 servings.*

Nutrition Information Per Serving

1 serving		% of U.S. RDA	
Calories	360	Vitamin A	4%
Protein, g	22	Vitamin C	10%
Carbohydrate, g	29	Calcium	8%
Dietary fiber, g	6	Iron	18%
Fat, g	20		
Cholesterol, mg	60		
Sodium, mg	1050		

Chuckwagon Soup

For a real southwestern treat, serve this hearty soup sprinkled with broken tortilla chips.

1 cup dried pinto beans, sorted and rinsed

3 cups water

1 tablespoon vegetable oil

1 pound beef stew meat

1 large onion, chopped (about 1 cup)

2 cups beef broth

1 jar (24 ounces) thick salsa

Heat beans and water to boiling in large Dutch oven. Boil 2 minutes; remove from heat. Cover and let stand 1 hour; drain.

Heat oil in Dutch oven over medium heat. Cook beef and onion in oil 8 to 10 minutes, stirring occasionally, until beef is brown. Stir in beans, broth and salsa. Heat to boiling; reduce heat.

Cover and simmer about 2 hours or until beef and beans are tender. *4 servings.*

Nutrition Information Per Serving

1 serving		% of U.S. RDA	
Calories	430	Vitamin A	12%
Protein, g	27	Vitamin C	4%
Carbohydrate, g	31	Calcium	8%
Dietary fiber, g	5	Iron	26%
Fat, g	24		
Cholesterol, mg	65		
Sodium, mg	2160		

Vegetable-Beef–Bulgur Soup

Bulgur adds a nutty flavor and chewy texture to this vegetable-beef soup. It is also a way to add more protein without extra meat.

1 tablespoon vegetable oil

1 pound beef boneless chuck, tip or round steak, cut into ½-inch cubes

2 cups beef broth

1 teaspoon salt

1 teaspoon chopped fresh or ¼ teaspoon dried marjoram leaves

1 teaspoon chopped fresh or ¼ teaspoon dried thyme leaves

⅛ teaspoon pepper

1 bay leaf

3 cups water

1 cup green peas

½ cup uncooked bulgur

3 medium carrots, sliced (about 1½ cups)

1 medium stalk celery, sliced (about ½ cup)

1 medium onion, chopped (about ½ cup)

1 can (16 ounces) whole tomatoes, undrained

Heat oil in Dutch oven over medium heat. Cook beef in oil, stirring occasionally, until brown. Stir in broth, salt, marjoram, thyme, pepper and bay leaf. Heat to boiling; reduce heat. Cover and simmer 1 to 1½ hours or until beef is tender.

Stir in remaining ingredients, breaking up tomatoes. Heat to boiling; reduce heat. Cover and simmer about 35 minutes or until carrots are tender. Remove bay leaf. *5 servings.*

Nutrition Information Per Serving

1 serving		% of U.S. RDA	
Calories	365	Vitamin A	100%
Protein, g	22	Vitamin C	10%
Carbohydrate, g	32	Calcium	8%
Dietary fiber, g	8	Iron	20%
Fat, g	19		
Cholesterol, mg	50		
Sodium, mg	930		

Chile Pork Soup

¼ cup vegetable oil

1 clove garlic, finely chopped

1 pound pork boneless shoulder, cut into ½-inch cubes

¼ cup all-purpose flour

1 medium onion, chopped (about ½ cup)

¼ cup chopped green chiles

1 tablespoon chopped fresh or 1 teaspoon dried oregano leaves

1 tablespoon chile powder

2 cans (16 ounces each) hominy, drained

1 can (15 to 16 ounces) pinto beans, rinsed and drained

3 cups chicken broth

½ teaspoon salt

¼ teaspoon pepper

¼ cup chopped fresh cilantro

Heat oil and garlic in 3-quart saucepan over medium heat until hot. Coat pork with flour. Cook pork in oil, stirring occasionally, until brown; remove from saucepan. Cook onion in same saucepan, stirring occasionally, until tender. Stir in chiles, oregano, chile powder, hominy and beans. Heat to boiling; reduce heat. Cover and simmer 10 minutes. Stir in pork, broth, salt and pepper. Heat to boiling; reduce heat. Cover and simmer 30 minutes. Stir in cilantro. *6 servings.*

Nutrition Information Per Serving

1 serving		% of U.S. RDA	
Calories	425	Vitamin A	12%
Protein, g	21	Vitamin C	10%
Carbohydrate, g	42	Calcium	6%
Dietary fiber, g	9	Iron	20%
Fat, g	23		
Cholesterol, mg	40		
Sodium, mg	1020		

Scandinavian Split Pea and Barley Soup

(Photograph on page 47)

If you are lucky enough to have a meaty ham bone on hand, use it in place of the chopped ham. Before serving, remove bone from the soup; cut off the ham and return to soup.

2 cups dried green split peas, sorted and rinsed

2 cups chopped cooked ham

½ cup uncooked regular pearled barley

8 cups water

1 teaspoon ground allspice

4 medium carrots, diced (about 2 cups)

1 large onion, chopped (about 1 cup)

1 medium stalk celery (with leaves), sliced (about ½ cup)

½ medium rutabaga, cubed (about 1 cup)

Mix all ingredients in Dutch oven. Heat to boiling; reduce heat. Cover and simmer 50 to 60 minutes or until peas fall apart and vegetables and barley are tender. *6 servings.*

Nutrition Information Per Serving

1 serving		% of U.S. RDA	
Calories	395	Vitamin A	100%
Protein, g	28	Vitamin C	10%
Carbohydrate, g	63	Calcium	6%
Dietary fiber, g	10	Iron	22%
Fat, g	8		
Cholesterol, mg	30		
Sodium, mg	490		

Old-fashioned Chicken Noodle Soup

Nothing is more comforting than homemade chicken soup. Made with thick, "dumpling" noodles, this version is a true classic.

Chicken and Broth (right)

2 cups all-purpose flour

½ cup water

2 tablespoons vegetable oil

½ teaspoon salt

2 medium carrots, sliced (about 1 cup)

2 medium stalks celery, sliced (about 1 cup)

1 small onion, chopped (about ¼ cup)

1½ teaspoons fresh or ½ teaspoon dried thyme leaves

Prepare Chicken and Broth; reserve cut-up chicken and broth. Mix flour, water, oil and salt in medium bowl. Stir in additional water, 1 tablespoon at a time, if necessary, until dough is stiff but easy to roll. Roll dough to ⅛-inch thickness on lightly floured surface. Cut into 1½ × ½-inch strips.

Add enough water to broth to measure 5 cups. Heat broth, chicken, carrots, celery, onion and thyme to boiling Dutch oven. Drop noodles, one at a time, into boiling broth; reduce heat. Cover and simmer about 15 minutes or until carrots are tender. Let stand uncovered 10 minutes. *6 servings.*

CHICKEN AND BROTH

3- to 3½-pound cut-up broiler-fryer chicken

4½ cups cold water

1 teaspoon salt

½ teaspoon pepper

1 medium stalk celery with leaves, cut up

1 medium carrot, cut up

1 small onion, cut up

1 sprig parsley

Remove any excess fat from chicken. Place chicken, giblets (except liver) and neck in Dutch oven. Add remaining ingredients; heat to boiling. Skim foam from broth; reduce heat. Cover and simmer about 45 minutes or until juice of thickest pieces of chicken runs clear. Remove chicken from broth; cool chicken about 10 minutes or just until cool enough to handle. Strain broth through cheesecloth-lined sieve. Remove chicken from bones and skin; cut up chicken. Discard bones, skin and vegetables. Skim fat from broth. Use immediately, or cover and refrigerate broth and chicken in separate containers up to 24 hours.

Nutrition Information Per Serving

1 serving		% of U.S. RDA	
Calories	340	Vitamin A	82%
Protein, g	28	Vitamin C	*
Carbohydrate, g	38	Calcium	4%
Dietary fiber, g	3	Iron	20%
Fat, g	10		
Cholesterol, mg	65		
Sodium, mg	630		

Hearty Chicken-Corn Chowder

3- to 3½-pound cut-up broiler-fryer chicken

6 cups water

1 medium onion, sliced

3 medium stalks celery (with leaves), finely chopped (about 1½ cups)

2 medium carrots, chopped (about 1 cup)

1½ teaspoons salt

2 cans (16 ounces each) cream-style corn

Egg Rivels (below)

Remove any excess fat from chicken. Place chicken, giblets (except liver) and neck in Dutch oven. Add water, onion, celery, carrots and salt; heat to boiling. Skim foam from broth; reduce heat. Cover and simmer about 45 minutes or until juice of thickest pieces of chicken runs clear.

Remove chicken from broth; cool chicken about 10 minutes or just until cool enough to handle. Remove chicken from bones and skin; cut up chicken. Discard bones and skin. Skim fat from broth. Stir chicken into broth. Stir in corn. Heat to boiling; reduce heat. Prepare Egg Rivels; sprinkle mixture over soup and stir in. Simmer uncovered 10 minutes. *8 servings.*

EGG RIVELS

1 cup all-purpose flour

¼ teaspoon salt

1 egg

Mix all ingredients, using fork, until mixture resembles cornmeal.

Nutrition Information Per Serving

1 serving		% of U.S. RDA	
Calories	285	Vitamin A	50%
Protein, g	23	Vitamin C	*
Carbohydrate, g	35	Calcium	6%
Dietary fiber, g	5	Iron	12%
Fat, g	8		
Cholesterol, mg	80		
Sodium, mg	830		

Chicken-Tortellini Soup

(Photograph on page 47)

3- to 4-pound cut-up broiler-fryer chicken

6 cups water

1½ teaspoons salt

1 teaspoon peppercorns

1 medium stalk celery (with leaves), cut into 1-inch pieces

1 medium carrot, cut into 1-inch pieces

1 medium onion, cut into fourths

2 sprigs parsley

1 bay leaf

2 cups water

2 cups uncooked dried, refrigerated or frozen cheese-filled tortellini (about 8 ounces)

2 medium zucchini or yellow summer squash, cut lengthwise in half and sliced

Remove any excess fat from chicken. Place chicken, giblets (except liver) and neck in

Dutch oven. Add 6 cups water, the salt, pepper-corns, celery, carrot, onion, parsley and bay leaf; heat to boiling. Skim foam from broth; reduce heat. Cover and simmer about 45 minutes or until juice of thickest pieces of chicken runs clear.

Remove chicken from broth; cool chicken about 10 minutes or just until cool enough to handle. Strain broth through cheesecloth-lined sieve. Remove chicken from bones and skin; cut chicken into bite-size pieces. Stir chicken into broth. Discard bones, skin and strained vegetables.

Stir 2 cups water into broth mixture. Heat to boiling. Add tortellini and zucchini. Heat to boiling; reduce heat. Cover and simmer about 20 minutes or until tortellini are tender. Sprinkle with chopped chives if desired. *8 servings.*

Nutrition Information Per Serving

1 serving		% of U.S. RDA	
Calories	210	Vitamin A	24%
Protein, g	23	Vitamin C	*
Carbohydrate, g	12	Calcium	6%
Dietary fiber, g	1	Iron	10%
Fat, g	8		
Cholesterol, mg	110		
Sodium, mg	650		

Lentil Soup

1¼ cups dried lentils, sorted and rinsed

3 cups water

1 tablespoon chopped fresh parsley

1 tablespoon beef bouillon granules

1 teaspoon salt

½ teaspoon ground cumin

3 medium carrots, sliced (about 1½ cups)

2 medium potatoes, cut into 1-inch cubes

1 medium onion, chopped (about ½ cup)

1 medium stalk celery, chopped (about ½ cup)

2 cloves garlic, finely chopped

Lemon wedges, if desired

Heat lentils and water to boiling in Dutch oven; reduce heat. Cover and cook about 30 minutes or until lentils are almost tender. Stir in remaining ingredients except lemon wedges. Cover and cook about 20 minutes or until potatoes are tender. Serve with lemon wedges. *4 servings.*

Nutrition Information Per Serving

1 serving		% of U.S. RDA	
Calories	260	Vitamin A	100%
Protein, g	18	Vitamin C	8%
Carbohydrate, g	57	Calcium	8%
Dietary fiber, g	12	Iron	36%
Fat, g	1		
Cholesterol, mg	0		
Sodium, mg	1540		

HOMEMADE QUICK BREADS

Making an easy dinner doesn't rule out a hearty loaf of home-baked bread when you use these easy, no-rise recipes. You'll love the combination of freshly baked bread with the stews, chiles and soups gathered here!

Chile Bread

2 cups all-purpose flour

2 teaspoons baking powder

½ teaspoon salt

½ teaspoon baking soda

½ teaspoon chile powder

1 cup shredded Cheddar cheese (4 ounces)

1 can (4 ounces) chopped green chiles, well drained

1 cup drained canned whole kernel corn

1 cup milk

1 tablespoon white vinegar

1 tablespoon vegetable oil

1 egg, beaten

Heat oven to 350°. Grease pie plate, 9 x 1¼ inches. Mix flour, baking powder, salt, baking soda and chile powder in large bowl. Add cheese and chiles; toss. Stir in remaining ingredients just until flour is moistened (batter will be lumpy). Pour into pie plate. Bake 40 to 45 minutes or until golden brown and toothpick inserted in center comes out clean. Remove from pie plate; cool on wire rack. *1 loaf (8 wedges).*

Nutrition Information Per Serving

1 wedge		% of U.S. RDA	
Calories	225	Vitamin A	6%
Protein, g	9	Vitamin C	10%
Carbohydrate, g	29	Calcium	18%
Dietary fiber, g	2	Iron	10%
Fat, g	8		
Cholesterol, mg	45		
Sodium, mg	620		

Chutney Bread

2½ cups all-purpose flour

½ cup granulated sugar

½ cup packed brown sugar

1¼ cups milk

3 tablespoons vegetable oil

1 tablespoon grated orange peel

3½ teaspoons baking powder

½ teaspoon salt

1 egg

¾ cup chutney

1 cup chopped nuts

Curry Spread (below)

Heat oven to 350°. Grease loaf pan, 9 × 5 × 3 inches. Mix flour, sugars, milk, oil, orange peel, baking powder, salt and egg in large bowl. Beat on low speed, scraping bowl constantly, until moistened. Beat on medium speed 30 seconds, scraping bowl occasionally. Stir in chutney and nuts. Pour into pan. Bake 60 to 65 minutes or until toothpick inserted in center comes out clean. Cool slightly; remove from pan. Cool completely on wire rack before slicing. Serve with Curry Spread. *1 loaf (24 slices).*

CURRY SPREAD

 2 teaspoons sugar

 2 teaspoons curry powder

 Dash of salt

 1 package (8 ounces) cream cheese, softened

Beat all ingredients until smooth.

Nutrition Information Per Serving

1 slice		% of U.S. RDA	
Calories	185	Vitamin A	4%
Protein, g	3	Vitamin C	*
Carbohydrate, g	23	Calcium	6%
Dietary fiber, g	1	Iron	6%
Fat, g	9		
Cholesterol, mg	20		
Sodium, mg	160		

Zucchini-Graham Bread

 3 eggs

 1 cup sugar

 ⅔ cup vegetable oil

 1 tablespoon vanilla

 2 cups packed shredded zucchini (about 2 medium)

 1⅔ cups graham cracker crumbs (about 22 squares)

 1½ cups all-purpose flour

 1 tablespoon ground cinnamon

 2 teaspoons baking soda

 ½ teaspoon baking powder

 1 cup chopped walnuts

Heat oven to 325°. Grease and flour 2 loaf pans, 9 × 5 × 3 or 8½ × 4½ × 2½ inches. Beat eggs slightly in large bowl. Mix in sugar, oil and vanilla. Stir in zucchini. Gradually stir in cracker crumbs, flour, cinnamon, baking soda and baking powder. Stir in walnuts. Pour into pans.

Bake 50 to 60 minutes or until toothpick inserted in center comes out clean. Cool 10 minutes; remove from pans. Cool completely on wire rack before slicing. Store tightly wrapped in refrigerator. *2 loaves (24 slices each).*

Nutrition Information Per Serving

1 slice		% of U.S. RDA	
Calories	85	Vitamin A	*
Protein, g	1	Vitamin C	*
Carbohydrate, g	9	Calcium	*
Dietary fiber, g	1	Iron	2%
Fat, g	5		
Cholesterol, mg	15		
Sodium, mg	65		

New Potato–Fish Chowder

3 cups water

1 teaspoon chopped fresh or ½ teaspoon dried thyme leaves

½ teaspoon salt

¼ teaspoon pepper

1 medium onion, chopped (about ½ cup)

18 small new potatoes (about 2¼ pounds), cut into fourths

3 medium carrots, thinly sliced (about 1½ cups)

1½ pounds lean white fish fillets, cut into 1-inch pieces

1 cup green peas

3 cups half-and-half or milk

Heat water, thyme, salt, pepper and onion to boiling in Dutch oven. Stir in potatoes and carrots. Heat to boiling; reduce heat. Cover and simmer about 10 minutes or until potatoes are almost tender.

Stir in fish and peas. Heat to boiling; reduce heat. Cover and simmer 6 to 8 minutes, gently stirring after 4 minutes, until fish flakes easily with fork. Gently stir in half-and-half. Heat until hot. *6 servings.*

Nutrition Information Per Serving

1 serving		% of U.S. RDA	
Calories	520	Vitamin A	94%
Protein, g	31	Vitamin C	20%
Carbohydrate, g	69	Calcium	18%
Dietary fiber, g	6	Iron	10%
Fat, g	16		
Cholesterol, mg	105		
Sodium, mg	370		

Bean and Pasta Soup

1¼ cups dried great northern or navy beans, sorted and rinsed

6 cups water

1 large onion, chopped (about 1 cup)

2 medium stalks celery, sliced (about 1 cup)

2 cloves garlic, chopped

2 cups chopped fully cooked smoked ham

2 teaspoons beef bouillon granules

½ teaspoon salt

¼ teaspoon pepper

1 cup uncooked elbow macaroni

2 medium tomatoes, chopped (about 1½ cups)

Heat beans and water to boiling in Dutch oven. Boil 2 minutes; remove from heat. Cover and let stand 1 hour.

Stir onion, celery, garlic, ham, bouillon granules, salt and pepper into beans. Heat to boiling; reduce heat. Cover and simmer about 2 hours or until beans are tender (do not boil or beans will burst). Skim fat if necessary. Stir macaroni and tomatoes into soup. Cover and simmer 10 to 15 minutes or until macaroni is tender. *6 servings.*

Nutrition Information Per Serving

1 serving		% of U.S. RDA	
Calories	265	Vitamin A	2%
Protein, g	21	Vitamin C	10%
Carbohydrate, g	34	Calcium	10%
Dietary fiber, g	7	Iron	26%
Fat, g	8		
Cholesterol, mg	35		
Sodium, mg	1070		

Wild Rice Chowder

(Photograph on page 48)

For a special treat, stir 1 tablespoon dry sherry, brandy or sauterne into each serving of this rich soup. If crimini or shiitake mushrooms are not available, button mushrooms are also delicious.

3 cups water

1 cup uncooked wild rice

2 tablespoons margarine or butter

2 cups fresh crimini or shiitake mushrooms, sliced

1/4 cup finely chopped shallots

1/4 cup diced celery

2 cups chopped smoked turkey breast (about 1/2 pound)

2 cups chicken broth

2 tablespoons chopped fresh or 2 teaspoons dried chervil leaves

2 tablespoons all-purpose flour

1/4 cup water

1 1/4 cups half-and-half

Heat 3 cups water and the wild rice to boiling in 3-quart saucepan; reduce heat. Cover and simmer 15 minutes; drain and reserve.

Heat margarine in same saucepan over medium heat until melted. Cook mushrooms, shallots and celery in margarine about 3 minutes, stirring occasionally, until crisp-tender. Stir in wild rice, turkey, broth and chervil. Heat to boiling; reduce heat. Cover and simmer 15 to 20 minutes or until rice is tender. Mix flour and 1/4 cup water; stir into soup. Heat to boiling; boil 1 minute, stirring frequently. Stir in half-and-half. Heat thoroughly but do not boil. *4 servings.*

Nutrition Information Per Serving

1 serving		% of U.S. RDA	
Calories	450	Vitamin A	20%
Protein, g	25	Vitamin C	4%
Carbohydrate, g	49	Calcium	12%
Dietary fiber, g	4	Iron	20%
Fat, g	19		
Cholesterol, mg	55		
Sodium, mg	1330		

Keeping Take-along Foods Hot and Cold

When bringing along food, it is important to maintain proper temperature for food safety reasons. We can rely on insulated coolers and thermoses to keep foods at their proper temperature for several hours. Before transferring foods to storage containers, make certain they are either thoroughly heated or thoroughly chilled. Do not pack partially cooked foods.

• Thermoses should be preheated or chilled for at least thirty minutes before adding food. To preheat, pour boiling or very hot water in thermos and replace top. To cool a thermos, fill with ice water and replace top. Insulated coolers can be chilled by filling with ice water or ice cubes. Close the cooler lid and allow to chill for forty-five minutes to one hour.

• Keep hot and cold foods separated.

• Several towels or layers of newspaper can be wrapped around hot food containers to offer more insulation.

• Frozen ice packs or bags of ice should be packed around or on top of cold foods.

• Try not to open thermoses and coolers until you are ready to eat.

Golden Peanut Chicken Soup

(Photograph on page 42)

1 tablespoon olive or vegetable oil

1 large onion, chopped (about 1 cup)

3 cloves garlic, finely chopped

2 large skinless boneless chicken breast halves (about ¾ pound), cubed

2 medium sweet potatoes or yams, peeled and cubed (about 3 cups)

2 cups chicken broth

1 cup water

½ teaspoon salt

½ teaspoon pepper

½ teaspoon red pepper sauce

½ cup uncooked orzo (rosamarina) or other small pasta

1 medium yellow bell pepper, cut into 1-inch squares

½ cup creamy peanut butter

1 jar (2 ounces) sliced pimientos, drained

Heat oil in Dutch oven over medium-high heat. Cook onion, garlic and chicken in oil 8 to 10 minutes, stirring occasionally, until chicken is white. Stir in sweet potatoes, broth, water, salt, pepper and pepper sauce. Heat to boiling; reduce heat. Cover and simmer 20 to 25 minutes or until sweet potatoes are tender. Stir in orzo and bell pepper. Heat to boiling; reduce heat. Cover and simmer 10 to 12 minutes or until orzo is tender. Stir in peanut butter and pimientos. Heat thoroughly. *4 servings.*

Nutrition Information Per Serving

1 serving		% of U.S. RDA	
Calories	450	Vitamin A	26%
Protein, g	32	Vitamin C	20%
Carbohydrate, g	33	Calcium	4%
Dietary fiber, g	4	Iron	16%
Fat, g	23		
Cholesterol, mg	45		
Sodium, mg	870		

CASSEROLES, POT PIES AND PIZZAS

South-of-the-Border Swiss Steak

(Photograph on page 81)

Once you've prepared this dish on the stovetop, just pop it into the oven and do as you please while it bakes.

2 tablespoons all-purpose flour

1 teaspoon chile powder

¼ teaspoon salt

1 pound beef boneless round steak, about ¾ inch thick

1 tablespoon vegetable oil

1 cup salsa

½ cup water

½ teaspoon sugar

1 large sweet potato or yam, peeled and cut into 1-inch cubes (about 2 cups)

1 package (10 ounces) frozen whole kernel corn, thawed

Heat oven to 350°. Mix flour, chili powder and salt. Sprinkle half of the flour mixture over one side of beef steak; pound in. Turn beef and repeat with remaining flour mixture. Cut beef into 4 serving pieces.

Heat oil in ovenproof Dutch oven over medium heat until hot. Cook beef in oil about 10 minutes, turning once, until brown on both sides; drain. Stir in remaining ingredients. Heat to boiling; remove from heat. Cover and bake about 1 hour or until beef is tender. Serve over hot cooked noodles if desired. *4 servings.*

Nutrition Information Per Serving

1 serving		% of U.S. RDA	
Calories	365	Vitamin A	78%
Protein, g	24	Vitamin C	10%
Carbohydrate, g	48	Calcium	4%
Dietary fiber, g	5	Iron	20%
Fat, g	11		
Cholesterol, mg	55		
Sodium, mg	860		

Beef and Bulgur Casserole

This hearty casserole will remind you of Greek moussaka. If you'd like a little extra zip, use ¾ teaspoon red pepper sauce.

1 pound ground beef or pork

1 small green bell pepper, chopped (about ½ cup)

1 medium onion, chopped (about ½ cup)

1 can (16 ounces) whole tomatoes, undrained

½ cup water

⅓ cup raisins

2 tablespoons chopped fresh or 2 teaspoons dried oregano leaves

1 tablespoon Worcestershire sauce

½ teaspoon salt

½ teaspoon red pepper sauce

1 cup uncooked bulgur

2 small yellow summer squash, cut lengthwise in half and sliced (2 cups)

⅓ cup coarsely chopped walnuts

Heat oven to 375°. Cook ground beef, bell pepper and onion in 10-inch skillet over medium heat about 5 minutes, stirring frequently, until beef is brown; drain.

Stir in tomatoes, water, raisins, oregano, Worcestershire sauce, salt and pepper sauce, breaking up tomatoes. Heat to boiling. Stir in bulgur; reduce heat. Cover and simmer 5 minutes. Stir in squash and walnuts. Spoon mixture into ungreased 2-quart casserole. Cover and bake 20 minutes; stir. Cover and bake about 15 minutes longer or until bulgur is tender and mixture is heated through. *4 servings.*

Nutrition Information Per Serving

1 serving		% of U.S. RDA	
Calories	555	Vitamin A	10%
Protein, g	29	Vitamin C	30%
Carbohydrate, g	67	Calcium	12%
Dietary fiber, g	14	Iron	30%
Fat, g	25		
Cholesterol, mg	70		
Sodium, mg	570		

Curried Beef Casserole

2½ cups uncooked wheel-shaped macaroni (about 6 ounces)

1 pound ground beef

1 medium onion, chopped (about ½ cup)

2 tablespoons margarine or butter

2 tablespoons all-purpose flour

1 tablespoon curry powder

½ teaspoon salt

¼ teaspoon crushed red pepper

2 cups milk

1 container (8 ounces) sour cream

½ cup dry-roasted peanuts

1 package (10 ounces) frozen mixed vegetables, thawed

Heat oven to 350°. Grease 2-quart casserole. Cook macaroni as directed on package; drain. Meanwhile cook ground beef and onion in 10-inch skillet over medium heat, stirring frequently, until beef is brown and onion is tender; drain. Remove beef mixture from skillet.

Heat margarine in same skillet over medium heat until melted. Stir in flour, curry powder, salt and red pepper. Cook, stirring constantly, until smooth and bubbly; remove from heat. Stir in milk. Heat to boiling, stirring constantly. Boil and stir 1 minute; remove from heat. Stir in sour cream and peanuts.

Mix macaroni, beef mixture, vegetables and sour cream mixture in casserole. Cover and bake about 45 minutes or until hot. *6 servings.*

Nutrition Information Per Serving

1 serving		% of U.S. RDA	
Calories	610	Vitamin A	48%
Protein, g	28	Vitamin C	10%
Carbohydrate, g	57	Calcium	18%
Dietary fiber, g	4	Iron	24%
Fat, g	32		
Cholesterol, mg	75		
Sodium, mg	600		

Beef and Potatoes au Gratin

3 medium potatoes, cut into ¼-inch slices (about 3 cups)

1 pound ground beef

1 medium stalk celery, thinly sliced (about ½ cup)

3 tablespoons margarine or butter

3 tablespoons all-purpose flour

1 tablespoon chopped fresh or 1 teaspoon dried chervil leaves

1 teaspoon prepared mustard

¼ teaspoon salt

¼ teaspoon pepper

2 cups milk

1¼ cups shredded process sharp American cheese (5 ounces)

3 tablespoons chopped fresh parsley

¼ cup dry bread crumbs

1 tablespoon chopped fresh parsley

2 teaspoons margarine or butter, melted

Heat oven to 375°. Heat 4 cups water to boiling in 2½-quart saucepan. Add potato slices. Heat to boiling; reduce heat to medium. Cook uncovered 8 to 10 minutes or until just tender; drain and reserve.

While potatoes are cooking, cook ground beef and celery in 10-inch skillet over medium heat, stirring frequently, until beef is brown; drain. Remove beef mixture from skillet and reserve.

Heat 3 tablespoons margarine in same skillet over medium heat until melted. Stir in flour, chervil, mustard, salt and pepper. Cook, stirring constantly, until bubbly; remove from heat. Stir in milk. Heat to boiling, stirring constantly. Boil and stir 1 minute. Stir in cheese until melted. Stir in 3 tablespoons parsley.

Layer half of the potatoes in ungreased 2-quart casserole. Layer with beef mixture and remaining potatoes. Pour cheese sauce over potatoes. Bake uncovered 20 to 25 minutes or until bubbly. Mix bread crumbs, 1 tablespoon parsley and 2 teaspoons melted margarine; sprinkle over potatoes. Bake about 5 minutes or until crumbs are brown and crisp. Let stand 5 minutes before serving. *4 servings.*

Nutrition Information Per Serving

1 serving		% of U.S. RDA	
Calories	645	Vitamin A	32%
Protein, g	34	Vitamin C	10%
Carbohydrate, g	35	Calcium	36%
Dietary fiber, g	2	Iron	20%
Fat, g	42		
Cholesterol, mg	110		
Sodium, mg	950		

Lamb and Lentil Casserole

2 slices bacon, cut into 1-inch pieces

1 tablespoon vegetable oil

1 pound lamb or pork boneless loin or shoulder, cut into ³⁄₄-inch pieces

1 cup dried lentils, sorted and rinsed

1 cup water

1 tablespoon packed brown sugar

1 tablespoon chopped fresh or 1 teaspoon dried thyme leaves

1 tablespoon chopped fresh or 1 teaspoon dried savory leaves

¹⁄₄ teaspoon salt

¹⁄₄ teaspoon pepper

1 large onion, cut in half and sliced

3 medium carrots, thinly sliced (about 1¹⁄₂ cups)

1 can (14¹⁄₂ ounces) stewed tomatoes

1 can (8 ounces) tomato sauce

Heat oven to 350°. Cook bacon in Dutch oven over medium heat, stirring occasionally, until crisp. Remove bacon with slotted spoon and drain. Drain fat from Dutch oven. Heat oil in same Dutch oven over medium heat until hot. Cook lamb in oil, stirring frequently, until brown; drain.

Stir in bacon and remaining ingredients. Heat to boiling; remove from heat. Spoon into ungreased 2-quart casserole. Cover and bake 50 to 55 minutes, stirring occasionally, until lamb and lentils are tender. *4 servings.*

Nutrition Information Per Serving

1 serving		% of U.S. RDA	
Calories	545	Vitamin A	100%
Protein, g	49	Vitamin C	30%
Carbohydrate, g	56	Calcium	10%
Dietary fiber, g	12	Iron	54%
Fat, g	19		
Cholesterol, mg	110		
Sodium, mg	900		

Fruit and Rice Lamb Chops

Using a diced fruit and raisin mixture is a great way to include a variety of dried fruits in a dish. However, you can also use only raisins for equally fine results.

2 lamb leg sirloin chops or 4 lamb rib chops, ³⁄₄ inch thick (about 1 pound)

1 tablespoon vegetable oil

3 cups frozen mixed French-cut green beans, broccoli, mushrooms and red pepper

³⁄₄ cup uncooked regular long grain rice

¹⁄₄ cup sliced green onions (2 to 3 medium)

¹⁄₄ cup diced dried fruit and raisin mixture

1 cup chicken broth

1 tablespoon soy sauce

¹⁄₂ teaspoon salt

¹⁄₂ teaspoon ground coriander

¹⁄₂ teaspoon ground ginger

¹⁄₄ teaspoon pepper

1 can (5¹⁄₂ ounces) apricot nectar

Heat oven to 350°. Cut each lamb leg sirloin chop into 2 serving pieces. Heat oil in 10-inch skillet over medium heat. Cook lamb in oil until brown on both sides. Remove lamb from skillet.

Mix remaining ingredients in same skillet. Heat to boiling; remove from heat. Spoon mixture into ungreased rectangular pan, 11 × 7 × 1½ inches. Place lamb on top. Cover with aluminum foil and bake about 50 minutes or until rice and lamb are tender. *4 servings.*

Nutrition Information Per Serving

1 serving		% of U.S. RDA	
Calories	435	Vitamin A	10%
Protein, g	22	Vitamin C	10%
Carbohydrate, g	50	Calcium	6%
Dietary fiber, g	4	Iron	24%
Fat, g	18		
Cholesterol, mg	60		
Sodium, mg	780		

Lamb and Eggplant Bake

1 pound ground lamb or beef

1 large onion, chopped (about 1 cup)

2 cloves garlic, finely chopped

1 can (15 ounces) tomato sauce

1½ cups cubed peeled eggplant

1 medium potato, peeled and cubed (about 1 cup)

1 teaspoon ground cinnamon

¼ teaspoon ground nutmeg

¼ teaspoon pepper

Parmesan Cheese Topping (right)

½ cup grated Parmesan cheese

¼ cup sliced ripe olives

1 tablespoon chopped fresh parsley

Heat oven to 350°. Cook lamb, onion and garlic in 10-inch skillet over medium heat, stirring frequently, until lamb is brown; drain. Stir in tomato sauce, eggplant, potato, cinnamon, nutmeg and pepper. Heat to boiling; reduce heat. Cover and simmer 20 minutes, stirring frequently, until eggplant and potato are crisp-tender.

Meanwhile, prepare Parmesan Cheese Topping; reserve. Stir cheese and olives into lamb mixture. Spoon lamb mixture into ungreased 2-quart casserole. Pour topping over hot lamb mixture. Bake uncovered about 30 minutes or until top is set. Let stand 10 minutes before serving. Sprinkle with parsley. *4 servings.*

PARMESAN CHEESE TOPPING

3 tablespoons margarine or butter

3 tablespoons all-purpose flour

⅛ teaspoon pepper

2¼ cups milk

2 eggs, slightly beaten

½ cup grated Parmesan cheese

Heat margarine in 1½-quart saucepan over medium heat until melted. Stir in flour and pepper. Cook over medium heat, stirring constantly, until mixture is smooth and bubbly; remove from heat. Stir in milk. Heat to boiling, stirring constantly. Boil and stir 1 minute. Gradually stir at least half of the hot mixture into eggs; stir back into hot mixture in saucepan. Boil and stir 1 minute; remove from heat. Stir in cheese.

Nutrition Information Per Serving

1 serving		% of U.S. RDA	
Calories	580	Vitamin A	32%
Protein, g	37	Vitamin C	10%
Carbohydrate, g	35	Calcium	52%
Dietary fiber, g	4	Iron	22%
Fat, g	34		
Cholesterol, mg	200		
Sodium, mg	1440		

Pork Chops with Beans and Rice

(Photograph on page 82)

You can make this dish as mild or as spicy as you wish. If you like your foods fiery hot, use hot chiles and salsa, or if you like a more tame dish, use the green chiles here and a mild salsa.

> *1 tablespoon vegetable oil*
>
> *4 pork loin or rib chops, about ¾ inch thick (about 1½ pounds)*
>
> *2 cans (14½ ounces each) stewed tomatoes*
>
> *1 can (15 to 16 ounces) navy or kidney beans, rinsed and drained*
>
> *1 can (4 ounces) chopped green chiles, drained*
>
> *1 cup uncooked regular long grain rice*
>
> *1 cup chicken broth*
>
> *1 teaspoon ground cumin*
>
> *¼ teaspoon salt*
>
> *½ cup salsa*
>
> *½ cup shredded Cheddar cheese (2 ounces)*
>
> *Sliced green onions*

Heat oven to 350°. Heat oil in 10-inch skillet over medium heat. Cook pork chops in oil until brown on both sides. Remove pork from skillet; drain. Mix tomatoes, beans, chiles, rice, broth, cumin and salt in same skillet. Heat to boiling; remove from heat. Spoon mixture into ungreased rectangular pan, 13 × 9 × 2 inches. Place pork on top. Cover with aluminum foil and bake about 45 minutes or until pork is tender. Spoon salsa over pork. Sprinkle with cheese. Bake uncovered 1 to 2 minutes or until cheese is melted. Sprinkle with onions.
4 servings.

Nutrition Information Per Serving

1 serving		% of U.S. RDA	
Calories	695	Vitamin A	26%
Protein, g	40	Vitamin C	50%
Carbohydrate, g	89	Calcium	20%
Dietary fiber, g	11	Iron	38%
Fat, g	25		
Cholesterol, mg	85		
Sodium, mg	1720		

Creamy Ham and Asparagus Bake

(Photograph on page 83)

When fresh asparagus is in season, this rich, creamy casserole is especially nice for supper or brunch.

> *1 container (8 ounces) sour cream*
>
> *⅓ cup mayonnaise or salad dressing*
>
> *¼ cup milk*
>
> *1 teaspoon prepared mustard*
>
> *¼ teaspoon ground red pepper (cayenne)*
>
> *2¼ cups cooked rice*
>
> *2 cups cubed fully cooked smoked ham*
>
> *1½ pounds fresh asparagus, cut into 1-inch pieces**
>
> *⅓ cup dry bread crumbs*
>
> *3 tablespoons slivered almonds*
>
> *2 tablespoons margarine or butter, melted*

*2 packages (10 ounces each) frozen asparagus cuts, thawed, can be substituted for the fresh asparagus.

Heat oven to 400°. Mix sour cream, mayonnaise, milk, mustard and red pepper in medium bowl. Stir in rice, ham and asparagus. Spoon mixture into ungreased rectangular pan, 11 × 7 × 1½ inches.

Mix bread crumbs, almonds and margarine; sprinkle over ham mixture. Bake uncovered about 30 minutes or until topping is golden brown and mixture is heated through.
4 servings.

Nutrition Information Per Serving

1 serving		% of U.S. RDA	
Calories	680	Vitamin A	24%
Protein, g	24	Vitamin C	20%
Carbohydrate, g	46	Calcium	14%
Dietary fiber, g	3	Iron	18%
Fat, g	46		
Cholesterol, mg	95		
Sodium, mg	1390		

Chicken Breasts Florentine

(Photograph on page 84)

4 ounces uncooked egg noodles (2 to 2½ cups)

3 tablespoons margarine or butter

3 tablespoons all-purpose flour

¼ teaspoon pepper

1 cup milk

1 cup chicken broth

1 package (10 ounces) frozen chopped spinach, thawed and squeezed to drain

¼ cup grated Parmesan cheese

¼ teaspoon ground nutmeg

4 skinless boneless chicken breast halves (about 1 pound)

¼ cup grated Parmesan cheese

Ground nutmeg

Cook noodles as directed on package; drain. Heat oven to 375°. Grease rectangular pan, 11 × 7 × 1½ inches. Meanwhile heat margarine in 2-quart saucepan over medium heat until melted. Stir in flour and pepper. Cook over medium heat, stirring constantly, until smooth and bubbly; remove from heat. Stir in milk and broth. Heat to boiling, stirring constantly. Boil and stir 1 minute.

Mix spinach, noodles, half of the sauce, ¼ cup cheese and ¼ teaspoon nutmeg. Spoon mixture into pan. Place chicken on top. Pour remaining sauce over chicken and spinach mixture. Sprinkle with ¼ cup cheese and additional nutmeg. Cover with aluminum foil and bake 30 minutes. Uncover and bake about 15 minutes longer or until light brown on top and juices of chicken run clear. *4 servings.*

Nutrition Information Per Serving

1 serving		% of U.S. RDA	
Calories	410	Vitamin A	54%
Protein, g	37	Vitamin C	4%
Carbohydrate, g	29	Calcium	30%
Dietary fiber, g	2	Iron	18%
Fat, g	17		
Cholesterol, mg	100		
Sodium, mg	730		

DELICIOUS SALADS

Salads add a fresh and welcome touch to casseroles, pot pies and pizzas. If you'd like to prepare these no-fuss salads even more quickly, look for pre-cut vegetables in your local supermarket, or at a salad bar.

Creamy Pear Coleslaw

3 cups shredded cabbage (about ½ medium head)

⅓ cup mayonnaise or salad dressing

2 tablespoons frozen (thawed) orange juice concentrate

¼ teaspoon ground nutmeg

⅛ teaspoon salt

2 pears, diced*

Grated orange peel

Toss cabbage and pears in large bowl. Mix remaining ingredients except orange peel; toss with cabbage and pears. Garnish with orange peel. *4 servings.*

*1 can (8½ ounces) sliced pears, drained and diced, can be substituted for the fresh pears.

Nutrition Information Per Serving

1 serving		% of U.S. RDA	
Calories	200	Vitamin A	2%
Protein, g	1	Vitamin C	32%
Carbohydrate, g	15	Calcium	4%
Dietary fiber, g	4	Iron	2%
Fat, g	15		
Cholesterol, mg	10		
Sodium, mg	180		

Snap Pea Salad

1 cup cooked sugar snap peas

1 cup cooked julienne strips carrot

1 cup julienne strips cucumber

¼ cup Italian dressing

4 cups bite-size pieces lettuce

Mix peas, carrot, cucumber and dressing in large bowl. Cover and refrigerate at least 30 minutes, spooning dressing over vegetables occasionally. Toss with lettuce. *4 servings.*

Nutrition Information Per Serving

1 serving		% of U.S. RDA	
Calories	100	Vitamin A	100%
Protein, g	3	Vitamin C	16%
Carbohydrate, g	9	Calcium	4%
Dietary fiber, g	4	Iron	8%
Fat, g	7		
Cholesterol, mg	0		
Sodium, mg	180		

Greek Salad

Vinegar Dressing (below)

1 medium head lettuce, torn into bite-size pieces

1 bunch romaine, torn into bite-size pieces

1 medium cucumber, sliced

1 bunch green onions, cut into ½-inch pieces

24 Greek or green olives

10 radishes, sliced

1 cup crumbled feta or chèvre cheese (4 ounces)

1 medium carrot, shredded

Toss all ingredients except cheese and carrot. Sprinkle with cheese and carrot. *6 servings.*

VINEGAR DRESSING

½ cup olive or vegetable oil

⅓ cup wine vinegar

1 tablespoon chopped fresh or 1 teaspoon dried oregano leaves

1 teaspoon salt

Shake all ingredients in tightly covered container.

Nutrition Information Per Serving

1 serving		% of U.S. RDA	
Calories	270	Vitamin A	38%
Protein, g	5	Vitamin C	16%
Carbohydrate, g	6	Calcium	16%
Dietary fiber, g	3	Iron	10%
Fat, g	25		
Cholesterol, mg	15		
Sodium, mg	970		

Asian Coleslaw

Sesame Dressing (below)

2 cups finely shredded Chinese cabbage (about ½ pound)

¼ cup chopped jicama

¼ cup chopped green bell pepper

¼ cup coarsely shredded carrot

Toss all ingredients. *4 servings.*

SESAME DRESSING

3 tablespoons rice or white wine vinegar

2 teaspoons sugar

2 teaspoons sesame seed, toasted

2 teaspoons soy sauce

1 teaspoon sesame oil

⅛ teaspoon crushed red pepper

Mix all ingredients.

Nutrition Information Per Serving

1 serving		% of U.S. RDA	
Calories	40	Vitamin A	24%
Protein, g	1	Vitamin C	20%
Carbohydrate, g	5	Calcium	4%
Dietary fiber, g	1	Iron	4%
Fat, g	2		
Cholesterol, mg	0		
Sodium, mg	200		

Brown Rice and Barley Chicken Medley

(Photograph on page 84)

Sweet and tangy dried apricots along with barley perk up chicken and rice. Chicken tenders are the tenderloin strips of chicken breasts. If you can't find tenders, cut skinless boneless chicken breast halves into 1-inch-wide strips.

> 1 tablespoon vegetable oil
> 1 pound skinless boneless chicken breast tenders
> 2 cups sliced mushrooms
> 2/3 cup uncooked quick-cooking pearled barley
> 2/3 cup uncooked quick-cooking brown rice
> 1/3 cup chopped dried apricots
> 1/4 cup sliced green onions (2 to 3 medium)
> 1 1/3 cups chicken broth
> 1 tablespoon chopped fresh or 1 teaspoon dried thyme leaves
> 1/8 teaspoon ground red pepper (cayenne)
> 1 large carrot, shredded (about 1 cup)
> 1 can (5 1/2 ounces) apricot nectar

Heat oven to 350°. Heat oil in 10-inch skillet over medium heat. Cook chicken in oil about 5 minutes or until light brown on all sides. Stir in remaining ingredients. Heat to boiling; remove from heat.

Spoon mixture into ungreased 2-quart casserole. Cover and bake about 30 minutes or until chicken is no longer pink in center and barley and rice are tender. *4 servings.*

Nutrition Information Per Serving

1 serving		% of U.S. RDA	
Calories	460	Vitamin A	76%
Protein, g	35	Vitamin C	4%
Carbohydrate, g	70	Calcium	6%
Dietary fiber, g	10	Iron	28%
Fat, g	9		
Cholesterol, mg	60		
Sodium, mg	350		

Chicken-Vegetable Strata

(Photograph on page 85)

Turn to this easy strata when you want a make-ahead dish that's ready to bake without last-minute fuss. If you prefer, you can also leave your bread untrimmed.

> 4 to 5 slices whole wheat or rye bread
> 1 1/2 cups cut-up cooked chicken or turkey
> 1 1/2 cups frozen mixed broccoli, green beans, onions and red pepper
> 1 cup shredded Cheddar cheese (4 ounces)
> 2 cups milk
> 1 1/2 teaspoons chopped fresh or 1/2 teaspoon dried oregano leaves
> 1 1/2 teaspoons chopped fresh or 1/2 teaspoon dried thyme leaves
> 1 teaspoon onion powder
> 1/4 teaspoon pepper
> 4 eggs, slightly beaten

Trim crust edges from bread slices and cut each bread slice diagonally into 4 triangles. Arrange half of the bread in ungreased square pan, 8 × 8 × 2 inches. Top with chicken and vegetables. Sprinkle with cheese. Top with remaining bread.

Mix remaining ingredients; pour over bread. Cover and refrigerate at least 2 hours but no longer than 24 hours, occasionally pressing bread down into egg mixture.

Heat oven to 325°. Cover pan with aluminum foil and bake 30 minutes. Uncover and bake about 45 minutes longer or until knife inserted in center comes out clean. Let stand 10 minutes before serving. *4 servings.*

Nutrition Information Per Serving

1 serving		% of U.S. RDA	
Calories	425	Vitamin A	22%
Protein, g	37	Vitamin C	4%
Carbohydrate, g	25	Calcium	38%
Dietary fiber, g	3	Iron	18%
Fat, g	21		
Cholesterol, mg	300		
Sodium, mg	500		

Baked Chicken Gumbo

3 slices bacon, cut into 1-inch pieces

4 skinless chicken thighs (about 1¼ pounds)

1 large green bell pepper, chopped (about 1½ cups)

1 large onion, chopped (about 1 cup)

1 medium stalk celery, chopped (about ½ cup)

3 cloves garlic, finely chopped

1 package (10 ounces) frozen cut okra, thawed

1 cup chicken broth

¾ cup uncooked quick-cooking brown rice

½ teaspoon pepper

¼ teaspoon ground red pepper (cayenne)

2 tablespoons chopped fresh parsley

Cook bacon in 10-inch skillet over medium heat, stirring occasionally, until crisp. Remove bacon with slotted spoon and drain. Drain all but 1 tablespoon fat from skillet.

Heat oven to 350°. Cook chicken thighs in bacon fat over low heat about 15 minutes or until light brown on all sides. Remove chicken from skillet.

Cook bell pepper, onion, celery and garlic in drippings in skillet about 3 minutes, stirring frequently, until vegetables are crisp-tender. Stir in okra, broth, rice, pepper and red pepper. Heat to boiling; remove from heat. Pour rice mixture into ungreased rectangular baking dish, 11 × 7 × 1½ inches. Place chicken on top. Cover with aluminum foil and bake 40 to 45 minutes or until juices of chicken run clear and rice is tender. Sprinkle with parsley and bacon. *4 servings.*

Nutrition Information Per Serving

1 serving		% of U.S. RDA	
Calories	295	Vitamin A	6%
Protein, g	22	Vitamin C	20%
Carbohydrate, g	38	Calcium	10%
Dietary fiber, g	6	Iron	14%
Fat, g	9		
Cholesterol, mg	50		
Sodium, mg	330		

Turkey, Carrot and Noodle Bake

Vegetables and herbs add garden-fresh flavor to this saucy casserole.

4 ounces uncooked egg noodles (2 to 2½ cups)

1 pound ground turkey or beef

1 medium onion, chopped (about ½ cup)

3 medium carrots, thinly sliced (about 1½ cups)

2 medium tomatoes, seeded and cut into bite-size pieces

1 jar (12 ounces) chicken or turkey gravy

1 container (8 ounces) sour cream

1 tablespoon chopped fresh or 1 teaspoon dried sage leaves

1 tablespoon chopped fresh or 1 teaspoon dried marjoram leaves

¼ teaspoon pepper

½ cup buttery cracker crumbs

⅓ cup chopped pecans or walnuts

2 tablespoons margarine or butter, melted

Heat oven to 375°. Cook noodles as directed on package; drain. Meanwhile cook ground turkey and onion in 10-inch skillet over medium heat, stirring frequently, until turkey is white; drain. Stir in carrots, tomatoes, gravy, sour cream, sage, marjoram and pepper.

Place cooked noodles in ungreased rectangular pan, 11 × 7 × 1½ inches. Gently fold in turkey mixture. Cover with aluminum foil and bake 30 minutes. Mix cracker crumbs, pecans and margarine; sprinkle over turkey mixture. Bake uncovered 5 to 10 minutes or until heated through. *4 servings.*

Nutrition Information Per Serving

1 serving		% of U.S. RDA	
Calories	650	Vitamin A	100%
Protein, g	35	Vitamin C	10%
Carbohydrate, g	43	Calcium	14%
Dietary fiber, g	5	Iron	28%
Fat, g	40		
Cholesterol, mg	140		
Sodium, mg	880		

Creative Toppers

Would you like to dress up your casseroles? Try these simple, satisfying finishing touches.

• Place a cookie cutter on baked casserole. Sprinkle crushed potato chips, tortilla chips or crackers inside the cutter; remove cutter.

• Using a cookie cutter, cut shapes from American or processed Swiss cheese slices; arrange over casserole. Bake an additional two to five minutes to melt cheese.

• Cut your favorite cheese into thin, ½-inch strips and form a lattice design on top of the casserole. Bake an additional two to five minutes to melt cheese.

• Arrange French-fried onions, bread crumbs, crushed croutons, crushed corn chips, crushed potato chips, crushed crackers or chow mein noodles around edge of casserole dish before baking.

• Sprinkle chopped bell peppers, jalapeño pepper rings, green onions, chives, sliced olives, chopped tomatoes or chopped fresh herbs on baked casserole.

• Top with homemade croutons: Trim crust from bread; cut bread into ½-inch cubes. Toast in 200° oven, stirring occasionally, until crisp and golden brown. Toss with melted margarine or butter and desired herbs.

Swiss Turkey Bake

If your family prefers green peas to artichoke hearts, use a 10-ounce package of frozen peas.

¾ cup uncooked regular long grain rice

1 package (9 ounces) frozen artichoke hearts, thawed

2 tablespoons margarine or butter

2 tablespoons all-purpose flour

¼ teaspoon salt

¼ teaspoon ground nutmeg

¼ teaspoon pepper

2 cups milk

1 cup shredded Swiss cheese (4 ounces)

2 cups cut-up cooked turkey or chicken

¼ cup sunflower nuts

¼ cup dry bread crumbs

1 tablespoon chopped fresh parsley or dried parsley flakes

1 tablespoon margarine or butter, melted

Heat oven to 350°. Cook rice as directed on package. Cut up any large artichoke hearts. Heat 2 tablespoons margarine in 2-quart saucepan over medium heat until melted. Stir in flour, salt, nutmeg and pepper. Cook over medium heat, stirring constantly, until smooth and bubbly; remove from heat. Stir in milk. Heat to boiling, stirring constantly. Boil and stir 1 minute. Stir in cheese until melted.

Stir cooked rice, artichoke hearts, turkey and nuts into sauce. Spoon mixture into ungreased 2-quart casserole. Mix bread crumbs, parsley and 1 tablespoon melted margarine; sprinkle over turkey mixture. Cover and bake 35 to 40 minutes or until heated through. *4 servings.*

Nutrition Information Per Serving

1 serving		% of U.S. RDA	
Calories	610	Vitamin A	22%
Protein, g	40	Vitamin C	6%
Carbohydrate, g	53	Calcium	48%
Dietary fiber, g	3	Iron	24%
Fat, g	28		
Cholesterol, mg	95		
Sodium, mg	980		

Baked Fish with Brown Rice–Vegetable Stuffing

(Photograph on page 86)

2 large carrots, shredded (about 2 cups)

1 large onion, chopped (about 1 cup)

1 cup uncooked regular brown rice

2 cups chicken broth

1 teaspoon Italian seasoning

¼ teaspoon pepper

¾ cup shredded zucchini

1 pound fresh or frozen (thawed) sole or other lean fish fillets

Salt

Lemon pepper

1 medium tomato, cut into thin slices

Heat oven to 350°. Mix carrots, onion, rice, broth, Italian seasoning and pepper in 1½-quart saucepan. Heat to boiling; reduce heat. Cover and simmer about 35 minutes, stirring occasionally, just until rice is tender. Stir in zucchini. Heat to boiling; remove from heat.

Spoon rice mixture into ungreased rectangular pan, 11 × 7 × 1½ inches. Place fish fillets in single layer on top. Sprinkle with salt and lemon pepper. Cover with aluminum foil and bake 20 to 25 minutes or until fish flakes easily with fork. Place tomato slices on fish. Bake uncovered about 5 minutes or until tomatoes are heated through. *4 servings.*

Nutrition Information Per Serving

1 serving		% of U.S. RDA	
Calories	310	Vitamin A	100%
Protein, g	27	Vitamin C	10%
Carbohydrate, g	48	Calcium	6%
Dietary fiber, g	6	Iron	10%
Fat, g	4		
Cholesterol, mg	55		
Sodium, mg	650		

Salmon-Macaroni Casserole

1⅓ cups uncooked medium shell or elbow macaroni (about 4 ounces)

3 tablespoons margarine or butter

3 tablespoons all-purpose flour

1 tablespoon chopped fresh or 1 teaspoon dried marjoram leaves

½ teaspoon pepper

2 cups milk

1 cup shredded process sharp American or Cheddar cheese (4 ounces)

2 cups cooked broccoli flowerets

1 can (14¾ ounces) red or pink salmon, drained, skin and bones removed, and flaked

½ cup shredded process sharp American or Cheddar cheese (2 ounces)

Heat oven to 350°. Cook macaroni as directed on package; drain. Meanwhile heat margarine in 1½-quart saucepan over medium heat until melted. Stir in flour, marjoram and pepper. Cook over medium heat, stirring constantly, until smooth and bubbly; remove from heat. Stir in milk. Heat to boiling, stirring constantly. Boil and stir 1 minute. Stir in 1 cup cheese until melted.

Mix cooked macaroni, broccoli, salmon and sauce in ungreased 2-quart casserole. Cover and bake 25 minutes. Sprinkle with ½ cup cheese. Bake uncovered about 5 minutes or until heated through. *4 servings.*

Nutrition Information Per Serving

1 serving		% of U.S. RDA	
Calories	625	Vitamin A	48%
Protein, g	41	Vitamin C	30%
Carbohydrate, g	50	Calcium	62%
Dietary fiber, g	4	Iron	22%
Fat, g	31		
Cholesterol, mg	100		
Sodium, mg	1470		

Seafood Jambalaya Bake

If you'd like to make this an all-shrimp dish, just omit the crabmeat and increase the shrimp to 1 pound.

¾ pound fresh or frozen raw medium shrimp (in shells)

1 package (6 ounces) frozen crabmeat, thawed and drained

2 tablespoons margarine or butter

2 medium stalks celery, sliced (about 1 cup)

1 large onion, chopped (about 1 cup)

2 cloves garlic, finely chopped

¾ cup uncooked regular long grain rice

1½ cups chicken broth

1½ tablespoons chopped fresh or 1½ teaspoons dried basil leaves

2 teaspoons lemon juice

½ teaspoon red pepper sauce

¼ teaspoon pepper

1 can (16 ounces) whole tomatoes, undrained

Peel shrimp. (If shrimp are frozen, do not thaw; peel in cold water.) Make a shallow cut lengthwise down back of each shrimp; wash out vein. Remove cartilage from crabmeat.

Heat oven to 350°. Heat margarine in 10-inch skillet over medium heat until melted. Cook celery, onion and garlic in margarine about 3 minutes, stirring frequently, until vegetables are crisp-tender. Stir in remaining ingredients, breaking up tomatoes. Stir in shrimp and crabmeat. Heat to boiling; remove from heat.

Spoon mixture into ungreased rectangular baking dish, 11 × 7 × 1½ inches. Cover with aluminum foil and bake 50 to 55 minutes, stirring twice, until rice is tender and liquid is absorbed. *4 servings.*

Nutrition Information Per Serving

1 serving		% of U.S. RDA	
Calories	310	Vitamin A	18%
Protein, g	23	Vitamin C	10%
Carbohydrate, g	40	Calcium	12%
Dietary fiber, g	3	Iron	22%
Fat, g	8		
Cholesterol, mg	120		
Sodium, mg	770		

Scallops Tetrazzini

6 ounces uncooked spaghetti, broken into 3-inch pieces

1 pound bay or sea scallops

1½ cups water

1 tablespoon lemon juice

3 tablespoons margarine or butter

2 cups sliced mushrooms

½ cup sliced green onions (about 5 medium)

3 tablespoons all-purpose flour

¾ teaspoon ground mustard

¼ teaspoon salt

¼ teaspoon pepper

¼ teaspoon paprika

2 cups milk

¼ cup grated Romano cheese

2 tablespoons dry sherry, if desired

¼ cup grated Romano cheese

Heat oven to 350°. Cook spaghetti as directed on package; drain. Meanwhile, cut sea scallops into fourths. Mix scallops, water and lemon juice in 1½-quart saucepan. Heat to boiling; reduce heat. Simmer uncovered 1 to 3 minutes or until scallops are white. Remove scallops from saucepan; reserve ½ cup liquid.

Heat margarine in same saucepan over medium heat until melted. Cook mushrooms and onions in margarine about 3 minutes, stirring frequently, until vegetables are crisp-tender. Stir in flour, mustard, salt, pepper, and paprika. Cook over medium heat, stirring constantly, until bubbly; remove from heat. Stir in milk and reserved liquid. Heat to boiling, stirring constantly. Boil and stir 1 minute. Stir in ¼ cup cheese and the sherry.

Mix cooked spaghetti, scallops and sauce in ungreased rectangular pan, 11 × 7 × 1½ inches. Sprinkle with ¼ cup cheese. Bake uncovered

25 to 30 minutes or until heated through. *4 servings.*

Nutrition Information Per Serving

1 serving		% of U.S. RDA	
Calories	530	Vitamin A	26%
Protein, g	42	Vitamin C	10%
Carbohydrate, g	56	Calcium	44%
Dietary fiber, g	4	Iron	40%
Fat, g	17		
Cholesterol, mg	55		
Sodium, mg	960		

Rice and Bean Bake

1 cup uncooked regular long grain rice

1½ cups boiling water

1 tablespoon beef bouillon granules

1½ teaspoons chopped fresh or ½ teaspoon dried marjoram leaves

1 medium onion, chopped (about ½ cup)

1 can (15 to 16 ounces) kidney beans, undrained

1 package (10 ounces) frozen baby lima beans, thawed

½ cup shredded Cheddar cheese (2 ounces)

Heat oven to 350°. Mix all ingredients except cheese in ungreased 2-quart casserole. Cover and bake 60 to 65 minutes or until liquid is absorbed; stir. Sprinkle with cheese. *4 servings.*

Nutrition Information Per Serving

1 serving		% of U.S. RDA	
Calories	420	Vitamin A	4%
Protein, g	22	Vitamin C	10%
Carbohydrate, g	83	Calcium	14%
Dietary fiber, g	14	Iron	36%
Fat, g	6		
Cholesterol, mg	15		
Sodium, mg	1360		

▲ *South-of-the-Border Swiss Steak* (Recipe on page 65)

▲ *Creamy Ham and Asparagus Bake* (Recipe on page 70)

◄ *Pork Chops with Beans and Rice* (Recipe on page 70)

▲ *Chicken-Vegetable Strata* (Recipe on page 74)

◄ *Chicken Breasts Florentine* (Recipe on page 71); ***Brown Rice and Barley Chicken Medley*** (Recipe on page 74)

▲ *Four-Cheese and Vegetable Lasagne* (Recipe on page 97);
   Festive Garlic Bread (Recipe on page 118)

◄ *Baked Fish with Brown Rice-Vegetable Stuffing* (Recipe on page 78)

▲ *Curried Chicken Pot Pies* (Recipe on page 103)

◄ *Corn Bread-topped Sausage Pie* (Recipe on page 101)

▲ *Southwestern Pork Salad* (Recipe on page 114)

◄ *Mexican Pan Pizzas* (Recipe on page 105); *Individual Peasant Pizzas*
(Recipe on page 108)

▲ *Italian Bread Salad* (Recipe on page 116); *Southern Chicken Salad* (Recipe on page 117)

◄ *Vegetable-Pasta Salad* (Recipe on page 115)

93

▲ *Citrus Shrimp Salad* (Recipe on page 123); *Lemon English Muffin* (Recipe on page 118)

◄ *Tomato-Tortellini Salad* (Recipe on page 122)

Black Bean Salad (Recipe on page 124) ▶

Four-Cheese and Vegetable Lasagne

(Photograph on page 87)

Parmesan Sauce (right)

1 container (12 ounces) ricotta cheese or creamed cottage cheese (1½ cups)

¼ cup sliced green onions (2 to 3 medium)

½ cup milk

2 tablespoons grated Romano cheese

1 egg, beaten

2 medium zucchini, sliced

2 large carrots, cut in half lengthwise and thinly sliced

9 uncooked lasagne noodles (about 8 ounces)

1½ cups shredded white Cheddar cheese (6 ounces)

Heat oven to 350°. Prepare Parmesan Sauce. Mix ricotta cheese, onions, milk, Romano cheese and egg. Mix zucchini and carrots in separate bowl.

Spread one-third of the sauce in ungreased rectangular baking dish, 11 × 7 × 1½ inches. Top with 3 uncooked noodles, breaking to fit. Spread half of the ricotta mixture and half of the zucchini mixture over noodles. Sprinkle with one-third of the Cheddar cheese. Repeat with 3 noodles, remaining ricotta mixture, remaining zucchini mixture, one-third of the sauce and one-third of the Cheddar cheese. Top with remaining noodles, sauce and Cheddar cheese. Cover with aluminum foil and bake 35 minutes. Uncover and bake about 15 minutes longer or until noodles are done. Let stand 15 minutes before cutting. *6 servings.*

PARMESAN SAUCE

2 tablespoons margarine or butter

2 tablespoons all-purpose flour

1 tablespoon chopped fresh or 1 teaspoon dried basil leaves

¼ teaspoon pepper

2 cups milk

½ cup grated Parmesan cheese

Heat margarine in 2-quart saucepan over medium heat until melted. Stir in flour, basil and pepper. Cook over medium heat, stirring constantly, until smooth and bubbly; remove from heat. Stir in milk. Heat to boiling, stirring constantly. Boil and stir 1 minute. Stir in cheese.

Nutrition Information Per Serving

1 serving		% of U.S. RDA	
Calories	480	Vitamin A	84%
Protein, g	27	Vitamin C	8%
Carbohydrate, g	41	Calcium	58%
Dietary fiber, g	4	Iron	16%
Fat, g	25		
Cholesterol, mg	130		
Sodium, mg	710		

Baked Cauliflower and Chile Beans

1 cup uncooked instant rice

6 slices bacon, crisply cooked and crumbled

2 cans (15 to 16 ounces each) hot chile beans, undrained

1 package (16 ounces) frozen cauliflower, thawed

8 ounces Mexican-style process cheese spread loaf, cut into cubes

Heat oven to 350°. Mix all ingredients except cheese in ungreased 3-quart casserole. Sprinkle with cheese. Cover and bake about 1 hour or until rice and cauliflower are tender. *6 servings.*

Nutrition Information Per Serving

1 serving		% of U.S. RDA	
Calories	325	Vitamin A	14%
Protein, g	18	Vitamin C	30%
Carbohydrate, g	41	Calcium	26%
Dietary fiber, g	7	Iron	20%
Fat, g	13		
Cholesterol, mg	30		
Sodium, mg	1310		

Vegetable Brunch Omelet

Broccoli slaw is a preshredded mixture available in the produce section. Shredded cabbage can be used in its place.

1 cup sliced mushrooms

1 cup broccoli slaw

1/3 cup chicken broth

2 tablespoons uncooked bulgur

1 tablespoon margarine or butter

3/4 cup shredded Fontina cheese (3 ounces)

1/2 cup milk

1 tablespoon chopped fresh or 1 teaspoon dried chervil leaves

1/4 teaspoon salt

1/4 teaspoon pepper

8 eggs

Heat oven to 325°. Heat mushrooms, broccoli slaw, broth and bulgur to boiling in 1-quart saucepan; reduce heat. Cover and simmer about 12 minutes, stirring occasionally, until bulgur is tender. Drain any remaining liquid.

Heat margarine in square baking dish, 8 × 8 × 2 inches, in oven until melted. Tilt dish to coat bottom. Beat remaining ingredients in large bowl until blended. Stir in mushroom mixture. Pour into dish. Bake 35 to 40 minutes or just until eggs are set. Let stand 2 minutes before serving. *6 servings.*

Nutrition Information Per Serving

1 serving		% of U.S. RDA	
Calories	200	Vitamin A	24%
Protein, g	14	Vitamin C	10%
Carbohydrate, g	9	Calcium	18%
Dietary fiber, g	2	Iron	10%
Fat, g	13		
Cholesterol, mg	300		
Sodium, mg	340		

Beef Polenta Pie

Cornmeal makes an attractive polenta crust for this main-dish pie. For a complete dinner, just add a crisp green salad and crusty bread.

½ cup cornmeal

½ cup cold water

1½ cups boiling water

¼ teaspoon salt

½ cup grated Parmesan cheese

½ pound ground beef

1 package (10 ounces) frozen chopped spinach, thawed and squeezed to drain

1 jar (14 ounces) spaghetti sauce

1½ teaspoons chopped fresh or ½ teaspoon dried marjoram leaves

½ cup shredded mozzarella cheese (2 ounces)

Grease pie plate, 9 × 1¼ inches. Mix cornmeal and cold water in 1-quart saucepan. Stir in boiling water and salt. Cook over medium-high heat, stirring constantly, until mixture thickens and boils; reduce heat. Cover and simmer 10 minutes, stirring occasionally; remove from heat. Stir in Parmesan cheese until smooth. Spread on bottom and up side of pie plate. Cover and refrigerate at least 4 hours until completely firm.

Heat oven to 350°. Cover cornmeal mixture in pie plate with aluminum foil; bake 30 minutes. Meanwhile, cook ground beef in 10-inch skillet over medium heat, stirring frequently, until brown; drain. Stir spinach, spaghetti sauce and marjoram into beef.

Spoon beef mixture into polenta shell. Cover and bake 25 to 30 minutes or until heated through. Sprinkle with mozzarella cheese. Bake uncovered about 5 minutes or until cheese is melted. Let stand 10 minutes before cutting. *4 servings.*

Nutrition Information Per Serving

1 serving		% of U.S. RDA	
Calories	325	Vitamin A	46%
Protein, g	21	Vitamin C	10%
Carbohydrate, g	26	Calcium	36%
Dietary fiber, g	4	Iron	20%
Fat, g	19		
Cholesterol, mg	50		
Sodium, mg	1140		

Reheating Foods in the Microwave

When reheating foods in the microwave, we recommend bringing the internal temperature to 140°F. The food is usually hot enough when the center of the bottom of the dish is warm. A temperature probe or microwave thermometer is helpful to determine whether the food is hot enough at its center. Do not leave a conventional thermometer in the food while microwaving; use it to check the temperature only after reheating.

Moist foods reheat best, and covering foods adds speed and even heating. Pizzas and other crisp or crunchy foods reheat best when heated on a browning dish or a microwave rack, so the bottom doesn't get soggy.

For fastest heating reheat casseroles tightly covered. Stir or rotate once or twice during reheating. Casseroles that can't be stirred, such as lasagne, benefit from a standing time to allow the heat to equalize throughout the food. Individual servings heat more quickly than full recipes as they allow the microwaves to penetrate more deeply, heating the center more quickly. Casseroles containing eggs, cheese or large chunks of meat should be heated at a lower power setting to avoid overcooking.

Reuben Pot Pie

2 tablespoons margarine or butter

2 tablespoons all-purpose flour

1 teaspoon caraway seed

¼ teaspoon pepper

1 cup water

½ teaspoon beef bouillon granules

2 tablespoons Thousand Island dressing

2 cups frozen hash brown potatoes with onions and peppers, thawed

2 cups cut-up cooked corned beef

½ cup sauerkraut, drained and cut up

Rye Dumplings (below)

Heat oven to 400°. Heat margarine in 2-quart saucepan over medium heat until melted. Stir in flour, caraway seed and pepper. Cook over medium heat, stirring constantly, until smooth and bubbly; remove from heat. Stir in water and bouillon granules. Heat to boiling, stirring constantly. Boil and stir 1 minute. Stir in dressing until smooth. Stir in potatoes, corned beef and sauerkraut. Heat through.

Prepare Rye Dumplings. Spoon hot beef mixture into ungreased square baking dish, 8 × 8 × 2 inches. Drop ¼ batter onto the center of each fourth of the corned beef mixture. Bake 15 to 20 minutes or until golden brown. *4 servings.*

RYE DUMPLINGS

2 tablespoons margarine or butter

½ cup all-purpose flour

¼ cup rye flour

1 tablespoon packed brown sugar

1 teaspoon baking powder

Dash of salt

1 egg, beaten

2 tablespoons milk

Cut margarine into flours, brown sugar, baking powder and salt with pastry blender in medium bowl until mixture resembles fine crumbs. Stir in egg and milk.

Nutrition Information Per Serving

1 serving		% of U.S. RDA	
Calories	585	Vitamin A	18%
Protein, g	19	Vitamin C	10%
Carbohydrate, g	43	Calcium	12%
Dietary fiber, g	4	Iron	20%
Fat, g	39		
Cholesterol, mg	130		
Sodium, mg	1730		

Pork and Mashed Potato Pie

1 tablespoon vegetable oil

1 pound pork boneless loin or shoulder, cut into ½-inch pieces

2 medium carrots, sliced (about 1 cup)

2 medium stalks celery, sliced (about 1 cup)

1 medium onion, chopped (about ½ cup)

2½ cups sliced mushrooms (about 8 ounces)

¾ cup chicken broth

1 tablespoon chopped fresh or 1 teaspoon dried thyme leaves

1 tablespoon white vinegar

¼ teaspoon salt

¼ teaspoon pepper

½ cup apple juice

¼ cup all-purpose flour

1 cooking apple, cored and chopped

2 cups hot mashed potatoes

Heat oven to 375°. Heat oil in 3-quart saucepan over medium heat until hot. Cook pork in oil about 6 minutes, stirring frequently, until pork is brown. Stir in carrots, celery, onion, mushrooms, chicken broth, the thyme, vinegar, salt and pepper. Heat to boiling. Shake apple juice and the flour in tightly covered container. Gradually stir into pork mixture. Heat to boiling, stirring constantly. Boil and stir 1 minute. Stir in apple.

Spoon pork mixture into ungreased 2-quart casserole. Cover and bake 45 to 50 minutes, until pork is tender. Spoon mashed potatoes around edge of hot mixture in casserole. Bake uncovered 15 to 20 minutes or until potatoes are light brown. *4 servings.*

Nutrition Information Per Serving

1 serving		% of U.S. RDA	
Calories	455	Vitamin A	88%
Protein, g	39	Vitamin C	10%
Carbohydrate, g	49	Calcium	8%
Dietary fiber, g	6	Iron	32%
Fat, g	14		
Cholesterol, mg	105		
Sodium, mg	580		

Corn Bread–topped Sausage Pie

(Photograph on page 88)

1 pound bulk Italian sausage

1 cup sliced mushrooms (about 4 ounces) or 1 jar (4½ ounces) sliced mushrooms, drained

1 medium onion, chopped (about ½ cup)

1 small red or green bell pepper, chopped (about ½ cup)

2 cloves garlic, finely chopped

1 can (15 ounces) tomato sauce

1 package (10 ounces) frozen whole kernel corn, thawed

Corn Bread Topping (below)

Heat oven to 400°. Cook sausage, mushrooms, onion, bell pepper and garlic in 10-inch skillet over medium heat, stirring frequently, until sausage is brown; drain. Stir in tomato sauce and corn. Heat to boiling; remove from heat. Spoon mixture into ungreased 2-quart casserole.

Prepare Topping. Pour over hot sausage mixture, spreading evenly. Bake uncovered 20 to 25 minutes or until golden brown. *4 servings.*

CORN BREAD TOPPING

⅔ cup cornmeal

⅓ cup all-purpose flour

½ cup milk

1 tablespoon sugar

2 tablespoons vegetable oil

2 teaspoons baking powder

¼ teaspoon salt

1 egg

¼ cup shredded Monterey Jack cheese with peppers (1 ounce)

Mix all ingredients except cheese in medium bowl. Beat vigorously 30 seconds. Stir in cheese.

Nutrition Information Per Serving

1 serving		% of U.S. RDA	
Calories	730	Vitamin A	20%
Protein, g	36	Vitamin C	22%
Carbohydrate, g	59	Calcium	28%
Dietary fiber, g	7	Iron	26%
Fat, g	42		
Cholesterol, mg	200		
Sodium, mg	2220		

Chicken-Blue Cheese Pot Pie

Pastry (below)

1 pound ground chicken or turkey

3 tablespoons margarine or butter

3 tablespoons all-purpose flour

1 teaspoon chopped fresh or ½ teaspoon dried rosemary leaves

½ teaspoon lemon pepper

1½ cups milk

3 tablespoons crumbled blue or feta cheese

1 pound fresh asparagus, cut into 1-inch pieces*

Heat oven to 425°. Prepare Pastry. Roll pastry into 10-inch square; trim to make square even.

Cook ground chicken in 10-inch skillet over medium heat, stirring frequently, until brown; drain. Remove chicken from skillet. Heat margarine in same skillet over medium heat until melted. Stir in flour, rosemary and lemon pepper. Cook over medium heat, stirring constantly, until smooth and bubbly; remove from heat. Stir in milk. Heat to boiling, stirring constantly. Boil and stir 1 minute. Stir in cheese until melted. Stir in chicken and asparagus. Cook until thoroughly heated.

Spoon hot pork mixture into ungreased square baking dish, 8 × 8 × 2 inches. Place pastry square over pork mixture. Turn edges under and flute. Cut a few slits in pastry. Bake 30 to 35 minutes or until crust is golden brown. Let stand 5 minutes before serving. *4 servings.*

PASTRY

⅓ cup plus 1 tablespoon shortening

1 cup all-purpose flour

¼ teaspoon salt

2 to 3 tablespoons cold water

Cut shortening into flour and salt with pastry blender in medium bowl until particles are size of small peas. Sprinkle in water, 1 tablespoon at a time, tossing with fork until all flour is moistened and pastry almost cleans side of bowl (1 to 2 teaspoons additional water can be added if necessary). Gather pastry into a ball. Shape into flattened round on lightly floured cloth-covered surface.

*1 package (10 ounces) frozen asparagus cuts, thawed, can be substituted for the fresh asparagus.

Nutrition Information Per Serving

1 serving		% of U.S. RDA	
Calories	610	Vitamin A	22%
Protein, g	34	Vitamin C	10%
Carbohydrate, g	36	Calcium	18%
Dietary fiber, g	3	Iron	20%
Fat, g	38		
Cholesterol, mg	80		
Sodium, mg	430		

One-Dish Know-How

A baking dish is a square or rectangular shallow dish that is ovenproof. Use aluminum foil if a cover is required. A casserole is a round or oval-shaped dish with a tight-fitting cover. For best results, use the size casserole or baking dish specified in the recipe. If you have to substitute, use the following guide:

• For a 1- to 1½-quart casserole, use a square baking dish, 8 × 8 × 2 inches.

• For a 2-quart casserole, use a rectangular baking dish, 11 × 7 × 1½ inches.

• For a 3-quart casserole, use a rectangular baking dish, 13 × 9 × 2 inches.

Curried Chicken Pot Pies

(Photograph on page 89)

Individual pot pies give everyone his or her own meal in a dish! Purchase shredded Swiss cheese if you don't want to finely shred your own for the tasty crust. To cut the 5-inch circles of pastry, use the top edge of a 10-ounce custard cup as a guide. Cut the pastry about ½ inch out from the edge of the cup.

> *Swiss Cheese Pastry (right)*
> *2 tablespoons margarine or butter*
> *2 tablespoons all-purpose flour*
> *2 teaspoons curry powder*
> *½ teaspoon salt*
> *½ teaspoon onion powder*
> *1¼ cups milk*
> *1½ cups cut-up cooked chicken*
> *1½ cups frozen cut green beans, thawed*
> *1½ cups frozen whole kernel corn, thawed*

Prepare Swiss Cheese Pastry; divide into fourths. Roll or pat each fourth into a 5-inch circle.

Heat oven to 425°. Heat margarine in 2-quart saucepan over medium heat until melted. Stir in flour, curry powder, salt and onion powder. Cook over medium heat, stirring constantly, until smooth and bubbly; remove from heat. Stir in milk. Heat to boiling, stirring constantly. Boil and stir 1 minute. Stir in remaining ingredients. Heat to boiling; remove from heat.

Divide chicken mixture among 4 ungreased 10-ounce custard cups. Place pastry circle over filling in each custard cup. Turn edges under and flute. Cut several slits in each pastry circle.

Place pies on cookie sheet. Bake about 30 minutes or until crusts are golden brown.
4 servings.

SWISS CHEESE PASTRY

> *⅓ cup plus 1 tablespoon shortening*
> *1 cup all-purpose flour*
> *¼ teaspoon salt*
> *¼ cup finely shredded Swiss cheese (1 ounce)*
> *2 to 3 tablespoons cold water*

Cut shortening into flour and salt with pastry blender until particles are size of small peas. Stir in cheese. Sprinkle in water, 1 tablespoon at a time, tossing with fork until all flour is moistened and pastry almost cleans side of bowl (1 to 2 teaspoons additional water can be added if necessary). Gather pastry into a ball. Shape into flattened round on lightly floured cloth-covered surface.

Nutrition Information Per Serving

1 serving		% of U.S. RDA	
Calories	545	Vitamin A	14%
Protein, g	25	Vitamin C	*
Carbohydrate, g	41	Calcium	18%
Dietary fiber, g	4	Iron	16%
Fat, g	33		
Cholesterol, mg	55		
Sodium, mg	300		

Tarragon-Shrimp Pie

Buttermilk Topping (right)

3 tablespoons margarine or butter

1½ cups sliced leeks

3 tablespoons all-purpose flour

2 teaspoons chopped fresh or ½ teaspoon dried tarragon leaves

¼ teaspoon salt

¼ teaspoon ground nutmeg

1¾ cups milk

1 cup shredded process Swiss cheese (4 ounces)

2 cups cooked cauliflowerets (about ½ head)

¾ pound cooked shrimp or 1 package (12 ounces) frozen cooked shrimp, thawed

Prepare Buttermilk Topping. Pat topping dough into 7-inch circle. Cut into 8 wedges.

Heat oven to 400°. Heat margarine in 2-quart saucepan over medium heat until melted. Cook leeks in margarine over medium heat, stirring frequently, until tender. Stir in flour, tarragon, salt and nutmeg. Cook over medium heat, stirring constantly, until flour is completely absorbed; remove from heat. Stir in milk. Heat to boiling, stirring constantly. Boil and stir 1 minute. Stir in cheese until cheese is melted. Stir in cauliflower and shrimp. Heat to boiling; remove from heat.

Pour shrimp mixture into ungreased 2-quart casserole. Arrange wedges of topping, with points in center, on shrimp mixture. Bake uncovered about 20 minutes or until topping is golden brown. Let stand 10 minutes before serving. *4 servings.*

BUTTERMILK TOPPING

¼ cup (½ stick) margarine or butter

1 cup all-purpose flour

1½ teaspoons baking powder

¼ teaspoon cream of tartar

⅛ teaspoon salt

⅛ teaspoon baking soda

¼ cup buttermilk or sour milk

Cut margarine into flour, baking powder, cream of tartar, salt and baking soda with pastry blender in medium bowl until mixture resembles fine crumbs. Stir in buttermilk to form a dough. Turn dough onto floured surface; gently roll in flour to coat. Knead 10 times.

Nutrition Information Per Serving

1 serving		% of U.S. RDA	
Calories	570	Vitamin A	60%
Protein, g	35	Vitamin C	26%
Carbohydrate, g	41	Calcium	58%
Dietary fiber, g	3	Iron	32%
Fat, g	31		
Cholesterol, mg	200		
Sodium, mg	960		

Mexican Pan Pizza

(Photograph on page 90)

A real pizza pie! If you like, co-jack cheese can be used in place of the Monterey Jack and Cheddar cheeses.

Pan Crust (right)

½ pound ground pork or beef

1 teaspoon ground cumin

¾ cup salsa

2 teaspoons cornstarch

2 tablespoons sliced jalapeño chiles

½ cup shredded Monterey Jack cheese (2 ounces)

½ cup shredded Cheddar cheese (2 ounces)

Heat oven to 425°. Grease pie plate, 9 × 1¼ inches. Prepare Pan Crust. Pat crust dough onto bottom and up side of pie plate, using floured fingers. Cover and let rise in warm place about 20 minutes or until double. Bake 12 to 14 minutes or until light brown.

Cook ground pork and cumin in 10-inch skillet over medium heat, stirring frequently, until pork is no longer pink; drain. Mix salsa and cornstarch; stir into pork mixture. Cook about 1 minute, stirring constantly, until heated through and thickened. Spread pork mixture over crust. Top with chiles. Sprinkle with cheeses. Bake about 10 minutes or until heated through and cheese is melted. *4 servings.*

PAN CRUST

1 package regular active dry yeast

½ cup warm water (105° to 115°)

1⅓ cups all-purpose flour

1 tablespoon olive or vegetable oil

⅛ teaspoon salt

Dissolve yeast in warm water in medium bowl. Stir in remaining ingredients; beat vigorously 20 strokes. Let rest 5 minutes.

Nutrition Information Per Serving

1 serving		% of U.S. RDA	
Calories	450	Vitamin A	14%
Protein, g	23	Vitamin C	6%
Carbohydrate, g	39	Calcium	20%
Dietary fiber, g	3	Iron	20%
Fat, g	24		
Cholesterol, mg	65		
Sodium, mg	734		

Ovenproofing Cookware

Although made of various metals, many skillets and Dutch ovens have handles that are made of plastic and therefore cannot go directly into the oven. To make metal skillets or Dutch ovens with plastic handles ovenproof, wrap the handles with heavy-duty aluminum foil, completely covering all plastic. Now, these pieces will be safe for oven use.

Breakfast Pizza

Serve this hearty pizza with some mixed fruit and a beverage and you've got a great breakfast or brunch.

Whole Wheat Crust (right)

¹/₃ cup mayonnaise or salad dressing

¹/₃ cup sour cream

1¹/₂ teaspoons dried fines herbes

¹/₂ pound bulk pork sausage

4 eggs

¹/₂ cup milk

¹/₄ teaspoon salt

¹/₈ teaspoon pepper

1 medium zucchini, cut lengthwise in half and sliced

1 medium onion, chopped (about ¹/₂ cup)

1 cup shredded Swiss cheese (4 ounces)

Heat oven to 425°. Grease 12-inch pizza pan or cookie sheet. Prepare Whole Wheat Crust. Mix mayonnaise, sour cream and fines herbes. Cook sausage in 10-inch skillet over medium heat, stirring frequently, until brown. Drain and remove sausage, reserving 1 tablespoon drippings in skillet.

Pat crust dough into pizza pan or into 11-inch circle on cookie sheet, building up edge slightly, using floured fingers. Bake about 12 minutes or until golden brown. Beat eggs, milk, salt and pepper, using wire whisk.

Heat reserved drippings in skillet over medium heat until hot. Cook zucchini and onion in drippings, stirring frequently, until tender. Pour egg mixture into skillet. As mixture begins to set at bottom and side, gently lift cooked portions with spatula so that thin, uncooked portion can flow to bottom. Avoid constant stirring. Cook 3

to 4 minutes or until eggs are set throughout but still moist; remove from heat.

Spread mayonnaise mixture over crust. Top with sausage and egg mixture. Sprinkle with cheese. Bake about 10 minutes or until heated through and cheese is melted. *4 servings.*

WHOLE WHEAT CRUST

1 package regular active dry yeast

¹/₂ cup warm water (105° to 115°)

1 cup all-purpose flour

¹/₄ cup whole wheat flour

1 tablespoon olive or vegetable oil

¹/₈ teaspoon salt

Dissolve yeast in warm water in medium bowl. Stir in remaining ingredients; beat vigorously 20 strokes. Let rest 5 minutes.

Nutrition Information Per Serving

1 serving		% of U.S. RDA	
Calories	635	Vitamin A	18%
Protein, g	26	Vitamin C	*
Carbohydrate, g	39	Calcium	36%
Dietary fiber, g	3	Iron	18%
Fat, g	43		
Cholesterol, mg	290		
Sodium, mg	810		

Salami Pizza

The squash and celery add a refreshing flavor to this cheesy pizza. Any size salami will work, but cut large pieces into fourths.

Crust (right)

½ cup spaghetti sauce

1 tablespoon chopped fresh or 1 teaspoon dried basil leaves

1½ teaspoon chopped fresh or ½ teaspoon dried savory leaves

3 ounces sliced salami

1½ cups sliced yellow summer squash or zucchini

1 medium stalk celery, thinly sliced (about ½ cup)

1½ cups shredded provolone or mozzarella cheese (6 ounces)

Heat oven to 425°. Grease 12-inch pizza pan or cookie sheet. Prepare Crust. Pat crust dough into pizza pan or into 11-inch circle on cookie sheet, building up edge slightly, using floured fingers. Bake about 10 minutes or until crust starts to brown. Mix spaghetti sauce, basil and savory; spread over crust. Arrange salami and squash on sauce mixture. Sprinkle with celery and cheese. Bake about 15 minutes or until heated through and cheese is light brown. *4 servings.*

CRUST

1 package regular or quick-acting active dry yeast

½ cup warm water (105° to 115°)

1¼ cups all-purpose flour

1 tablespoon olive or vegetable oil

⅛ teaspoon salt

Dissolve yeast in warm water in medium bowl. Stir in remaining ingredients; beat vigorously 20 strokes. Let rest 5 minutes.

Nutrition Information Per Serving

1 serving		% of U.S. RDA	
Calories	400	Vitamin A	14%
Protein, g	19	Vitamin C	4%
Carbohydrate, g	38	Calcium	36%
Dietary fiber, g	4	Iron	20%
Fat, g	21		
Cholesterol, mg	50		
Sodium, mg	920		

Individual Peasant Pizzas

(Photograph on page 90)

Fast to make and fun to eat! When you can't find Havarti cheese, mozzarella or Monterey Jack cheese will work just as well.

¼ cup pesto

4 Italian flatbread rounds (6 inches in diameter)

1½ cups sliced roma (plum) tomatoes or small tomatoes

¼ cup cut-up Greek or ripe olives

2 cups shredded Havarti cheese (8 ounces)

Heat oven to 425°. Spread 1 tablespoon pesto on each flatbread round. Place flatbread rounds on ungreased cookie sheet. Sprinkle with cheese. Arrange tomatoes and olives on top. Bake 12 to 15 minutes or until heated through and cheese is melted. *4 servings.*

Nutrition Information Per Serving

1 serving		% of U.S. RDA	
Calories	520	Vitamin A	16%
Protein, g	23	Vitamin C	10%
Carbohydrate, g	51	Calcium	38%
Dietary fiber, g	3	Iron	16%
Fat, g	26		
Cholesterol, mg	60		
Sodium, mg	1060		

Flavorful Pizza Crusts

The flavor in pizza doesn't all have to come from the toppings! Stir one of the following items into your favorite pizza crust recipe the next time you cook. Now that's pizza, from the bottom up!

• 2 tablespoons wheat germ

• 2 tablespoons chopped fresh cilantro leaves

• 1 tablespoon snipped fresh chives

• 1 tablespoon chopped fresh or 1 teaspoon dried basil leaves

• 1 tablespoon chopped fresh or 1 teaspoon dried oregano leaves

• 1 teaspoon Italian seasoning

• Substitute olive oil for the vegetable oil.

• Substitute whole wheat flour for half of the all-purpose flour.

Deep-dish Turkey Pizza

If you're using a clear casserole, check the bottom crust to be sure it's golden brown.

> *Deep-dish Crust (right) or 1 loaf (1 pound) frozen bread dough, thawed*
>
> *1 package (10 ounces) frozen chopped broccoli*
>
> *1 cup cut-up cooked turkey*
>
> *1 cup shredded brick cheese (4 ounces)*
>
> *½ cup grated Romano or Parmesan cheese*
>
> *⅓ cup dry bread crumbs*
>
> *1 tablespoon chopped fresh or 1 teaspoon dried basil leaves*
>
> *1½ teaspoons chopped fresh or ½ teaspoon dried oregano leaves*
>
> *1 egg, beaten*
>
> *1 container (12 ounces) dry curd cottage cheese*
>
> *1 cup spaghetti sauce*

Prepare Deep-dish Crust. Cook broccoli as directed on package. Drain broccoli thoroughly, pressing out as much liquid as possible. Heat oven to 350°. Grease 2-quart casserole. Mix broccoli and remaining ingredients except spaghetti sauce.

Reserve one-third of the crust dough. Roll remaining dough into 13-inch circle on floured surface. Fit circle into bottom and up side of casserole. Spoon turkey mixture into crust.

Roll remaining dough into 8½-inch circle. Fit circle over turkey mixture. Fold bottom dough over top and pinch to seal. Brush crust lightly with water. Cover and bake 25 minutes. Uncover and bake 25 to 30 minutes longer or until crust is deep golden brown on top and all sides.

Let stand 10 minutes. Heat spaghetti sauce. Remove pizza from casserole. Cut pizza into wedges; serve with spaghetti sauce. Serve with additional grated Romano cheese if desired. *6 servings.*

DEEP-DISH CRUST

> *3 to 3½ cups all-purpose flour*
>
> *1 tablespoon sugar*
>
> *1 tablespoon shortening*
>
> *1 package regular active dry yeast*
>
> *1 teaspoon salt*
>
> *1¼ cups very warm water (120° to 130°)*

Mix 1¾ cups of the flour, the sugar, shortening, yeast and salt in large bowl. Add warm water. Beat on low speed 1 minute, scraping bowl frequently. Stir in enough remaining flour, ½ cup at a time, to make a dough that is easy to handle. Turn dough onto lightly floured surface; gently roll in flour to coat. Knead 8 to 10 minutes or until smooth and elastic. Place in greased bowl, and turn greased side up. Cover and let rise in warm place 35 to 45 minutes or until double. (Dough is ready if indentation remains when touched.)

Nutrition Information Per Serving

1 serving		% of U.S. RDA	
Calories	500	Vitamin A	20%
Protein, g	34	Vitamin C	10%
Carbohydrate, g	62	Calcium	32%
Dietary fiber, g	5	Iron	26%
Fat, g	15		
Cholesterol, mg	80		
Sodium, mg	960		

Seafood Pizza

A cornmeal pizza crust, dried tomatoes and caramelized leeks combine with crab for a truly sensational pizza.

½ cup cut-up sun-dried tomatoes (not oil-packed)

½ cup boiling water

Cornmeal Crust (right)

2 tablespoons margarine or butter

2 tablespoons all-purpose flour

¼ teaspoon salt

1 cup milk

2 tablespoons margarine or butter

1 teaspoon sugar

1 cup sliced leeks

1 cup cut-up cooked crabmeat or 1 package (6 ounces) frozen crabmeat, thawed, drained and cartilage removed

1 cup shredded mozzarella cheese (4 ounces)

Heat oven to 425°. Grease 12-inch pizza pan or cookie sheet. Mix tomatoes and boiling water; let stand to rehydrate tomatoes. Prepare Cornmeal Crust. Pat crust dough into pizza pan or into 10-inch circle on cookie sheet, building up edge slightly, using floured fingers. Bake about 10 minutes or until crust begins to brown.

Heat 2 tablespoons margarine in 1½-quart saucepan over medium heat until melted. Stir in flour and salt. Cook over medium heat, stirring constantly, until smooth and bubbly; remove from heat. Stir in milk. Heat to boiling, stirring constantly. Boil and stir 1 minute; remove from heat and reserve.

Heat 2 tablespoons margarine in 10-inch skillet over medium heat until melted. Stir in sugar.

Add leeks. Cook over medium-high heat, stirring constantly, until leeks are golden brown and caramelized; remove from heat and reserve. Drain tomatoes well.

Spread sauce over crust. Arrange caramelized leeks, tomatoes and crabmeat on sauce. Sprinkle with cheese. Bake 15 to 20 minutes or until heated through and cheese is melted. *4 servings.*

CORNMEAL CRUST

1 package regular active dry yeast

½ cup warm water (105° to 115°)

1 cup all-purpose flour

⅓ cup cornmeal

1 tablespoon olive or vegetable oil

⅛ teaspoon salt

Dissolve yeast in warm water in medium bowl. Stir in remaining ingredients; beat vigorously 20 strokes. Let rest 5 minutes.

Nutrition Information Per Serving

1 serving		% of U.S. RDA	
Calories	455	Vitamin A	38%
Protein, g	23	Vitamin C	10%
Carbohydrate, g	45	Calcium	34%
Dietary fiber, g	4	Iron	18%
Fat, g	22		
Cholesterol, mg	55		
Sodium, mg	620		

Mediterranean Pizza

Pizza Dough (right)

½ pound ground beef, cooked and drained

1 cup shredded mozzarella cheese (4 ounces)

½ cup crumbled feta cheese

½ cup Greek or ripe olives, cut up

1 tablespoon chopped fresh or 1 teaspoon dried basil leaves

1 small zucchini, thinly sliced

1 medium tomato, chopped (about ¾ cup)

Move oven rack to lowest position. Heat oven to 425°. Grease 12-inch pizza pan or cookie sheet. Prepare Pizza Dough. Pat dough into pizza pan or into 11-inch circle on cookie sheet, building up edge of crust slightly, using floured fingers.

Sprinkle remaining ingredients over dough. Bake 25 to 30 minutes or until crust is golden. Drizzle with 1 tablespoon olive oil if desired. *4 servings.*

PIZZA DOUGH

1 package regular or quick-acting active dry yeast

1 cup warm water (105° to 115°)

2½ cups all-purpose flour

2 tablespoons olive or vegetable oil

1 teaspoon sugar

1 teaspoon salt

Dissolve yeast in warm water in medium bowl. Stir in remaining ingredients; beat vigorously 20 strokes. Let rest 5 minutes.

Nutrition Information Per Serving

1 serving		% of U.S. RDA	
Calories	595	Vitamin A	8%
Protein, g	28	Vitamin C	4%
Carbohydrate, g	66	Calcium	32%
Dietary fiber, g	4	Iron	32%
Fat, g	26		
Cholesterol, mg	60		
Sodium, mg	1280		

Swiss Cheese Pizza

Easy Crust (right)

1 package (6 ounces) sliced Canadian-style bacon, chopped

1½ cups shredded Swiss cheese (6 ounces)

⅓ cup sliced green onions (about 3 medium)

2 eggs

2 tablespoons milk

⅛ teaspoon pepper

2 medium tomatoes, sliced

2 tablespoons grated Parmesan cheese

2 tablespoons chopped fresh parsley

Heat oven to 400°. Prepare Easy Crust. Place crust dough into ungreased 12-inch pizza pan or on ungreased cookie sheet, building up edge of crust slightly, using floured fingers. Sprinkle bacon, Swiss cheese and onions over crust. Beat eggs, milk and pepper with hand beater; pour evenly over top. Arrange tomatoes on top. Sprinkle with Parmesan cheese and parsley. Bake 20 to 25 minutes or until crust is golden and eggs are set. *6 servings.*

EASY CRUST

2 cups Bisquick® Original baking mix

⅓ cup very hot water

1 tablespoon vegetable oil

Mix all ingredients; beat vigorously 20 strokes. Turn dough onto surface generously dusted with baking mix; gently roll in baking mix to coat. Knead about 60 times or until smooth and no longer sticky. Roll dough into 12-inch circle.

Nutrition Information Per Serving

1 serving		% of U.S. RDA	
Calories	370	Vitamin A	10%
Protein, g	19	Vitamin C	10%
Carbohydrate, g	29	Calcium	38%
Dietary fiber, g	1	Iron	12%
Fat, g	20		
Cholesterol, mg	110		
Sodium, mg	1060		

MAIN-DISH SALADS

Beef-Potato Salad

1½ *pounds small new potatoes*

½ *pound sliced cooked roast beef, cut into thin strips*

1 small red onion, thinly sliced

1 small red bell pepper, thinly sliced

1 small bunch green leaf lettuce, torn into bite-size pieces

Red Wine Vinaigrette (right)

Place potatoes in 2-quart saucepan; add enough water to cover. Heat to boiling; reduce heat to medium. Cook uncovered 10 to 12 minutes or until potatoes are tender; drain. Cut potatoes into fourths. Mix potatoes and remaining ingredients except Red Wine Vinaigrette in large serving bowl. Toss with vinaigrette. Serve warm or cold. *4 servings.*

RED WINE VINAIGRETTE

¼ *cup olive or vegetable oil*

2 tablespoons red wine vinegar

1 tablespoon chopped fresh or 1 teaspoon dried thyme leaves

¼ *teaspoon salt*

⅛ *teaspoon ground red pepper (cayenne)*

Shake all ingredients in tightly covered container.

Nutrition Information Per Serving

1 serving		% of U.S. RDA	
Calories	485	Vitamin A	20%
Protein, g	17	Vitamin C	30%
Carbohydrate, g	38	Calcium	4%
Dietary fiber, g	4	Iron	24%
Fat, g	31		
Cholesterol, mg	50		
Sodium, mg	190		

Speedy Salad Savvy

Main-dish salads are terrific for weeknight meals because they can be assembled so quickly. Convenience products help you to have dinner ready when you are.

• Purchase prewashed, packaged lettuce combinations. Many types are available, from iceberg lettuce with shredded carrot and red cabbage to gourmet blends with radicchio (red-leafed Italian chicory), escarole (a variety of endive) and romaine lettuce. Prewashed spinach and coleslaw mixtures are also available.

• Purchase deli, canned, or cooked, frozen meats and seafood. Meat counters sell many types of pre-cut raw items such as stir-fry pieces and fajita strips.

• Purchase pre-cut fresh fruit and vegetables. Canned and frozen fruits and vegetables can be used as well.

• Purchase bottled salad dressings, packaged croutons and shredded cheese.

• Pasta, rice and grains can be cooked several days ahead of time and stored in the refrigerator.

Southwestern Pork Salad

(Photograph on page 91)

¾ pound pork tenderloin

¼ teaspoon salt

¼ teaspoon pepper

8 cups bite-size pieces mixed salad greens or 1 package (4 ounces) mixed greens

1 medium yellow bell pepper, sliced

½ pound mushrooms, sliced

1 can (15 to 16 ounces) black-eyed peas, rinsed and drained

Creamy Lime Dressing (below)

Heat oven to 350°. Place tenderloin on rack in shallow roasting pan. Sprinkle with salt and pepper. Insert meat thermometer horizontally so tip is in thickest part of pork. Bake uncovered 30 to 40 minutes or until thermometer registers 160° (medium doneness). Cool pork; cut into slices. Arrange greens, bell pepper, mushrooms, peas and pork on large serving plate. Serve with Creamy Lime Dressing. *4 servings.*

CREAMY LIME DRESSING

½ cup nonfat sour cream

¼ cup chopped fresh cilantro

2 tablespoons lime juice

2 tablespoons vegetable oil

¼ teaspoon salt

Mix all ingredients.

Nutrition Information Per Serving

1 serving		% of U.S. RDA	
Calories	330	Vitamin A	38%
Protein, g	36	Vitamin C	40%
Carbohydrate, g	30	Calcium	12%
Dietary fiber, g	11	Iron	36%
Fat, g	12		
Cholesterol, mg	90		
Sodium, mg	585		

Warm Spinach Salad

10 ounces spinach, torn into bite-size pieces (about 8 cups)

6 slices bacon

1 cup cubed fully cooked smoked ham

2 medium zucchini, cut into julienne strips

4 green onions, chopped

Hot Dressing (below)

Place spinach in large serving bowl. Cook bacon in 10-inch skillet over medium-high heat about 5 minutes or until crisp; drain and crumble. Drain fat from skillet. Cook ham, zucchini and onions in same skillet about 2 minutes, stirring occasionally, until onions are crisp-tender. Add bacon and ham mixture to spinach; toss. Prepare Hot Dressing in same skillet. Pour dressing over spinach mixture; toss. Serve warm. *4 servings.*

HOT DRESSING

½ cup water

¼ cup cider vinegar

1 tablespoon sugar

1 tablespoon flour

1 teaspoon Dijon mustard

½ teaspoon celery seed

Heat water and vinegar in skillet until hot. Stir in remaining ingredients. Cook and stir about 1 minute or until slightly thickened.

Nutrition Information Per Serving

1 serving		% of U.S. RDA	
Calories	195	Vitamin A	96%
Protein, g	14	Vitamin C	40%
Carbohydrate, g	14	Calcium	14%
Dietary fiber, g	4	Iron	24%
Fat, g	11		
Cholesterol, mg	30		
Sodium, mg	590		

Vegetable-Pasta Salad

(Photograph on page 92)

Making a pasta salad just doesn't get any easier than this—the frozen vegetables and pasta cook together in the same water. You can vary the ingredients in an almost endless number of combinations. Try combining different vegetables; various pasta shapes; cooked chicken, beef or pork; and your favorite salad dressing.

1 package (16 ounces) frozen mixed broccoli, cauliflower, pea pods and yellow peppers or other mixed vegetables

½ package (16-ounce size) rotini

2 cups cubed fully cooked smoked ham

½ cup Italian dressing

Heat 2½ quarts water to boiling in 4-quart saucepan. Cook vegetables and rotini in water 8 to 10 minutes or until rotini is tender; drain. Mix vegetables, rotini, ham and dressing. Cover and refrigerate about 1 hour or until chilled. *4 servings.*

Nutrition Information Per Serving

1 serving		% of U.S. RDA	
Calories	530	Vitamin A	78%
Protein, g	24	Vitamin C	30%
Carbohydrate, g	54	Calcium	6%
Dietary fiber, g	4	Iron	20%
Fat, g	26		
Cholesterol, mg	45		
Sodium, mg	940		

Italian Bread Salad

(Photograph on page 93)

Basil Vinaigrette (below)

2 teaspoons vegetable oil

1 small onion, thinly sliced

2 medium zucchini, cut lengthwise in half and sliced

½ pound mushrooms, sliced

1 small red bell pepper, cut into thin strips

3 cups cubed Italian bread, toasted

1 medium bunch red leaf lettuce, torn into bite-size pieces

¼ pound sliced pepperoni

½ pound mozzarella cheese, cut into ½-inch cubes

Prepare Basil Vinaigrette. Heat oil in 10-inch skillet over medium-high heat. Cook onion, zucchini, mushrooms and bell pepper in oil 4 to 5 minutes, stirring occasionally, until crisp-tender; drain. Place 1 cup of the bread cubes in large serving bowl. Drizzle with ¼ cup vinaigrette; toss to coat. Stir in vegetable mixture, remaining bread cubes and remaining ingredients. Toss with remaining vinaigrette. *6 servings.*

BASIL VINAIGRETTE

½ cup olive or vegetable oil

¼ cup red wine vinegar

¼ cup chopped fresh or 1 tablespoon dried basil leaves

¼ teaspoon salt

2 cloves garlic, crushed

Shake all ingredients in tightly covered container.

Nutrition Information Per Serving

1 serving		% of U.S. RDA	
Calories	440	Vitamin A	24%
Protein, g	17	Vitamin C	20%
Carbohydrate, g	16	Calcium	34%
Dietary fiber, g	2	Iron	14%
Fat, g	35		
Cholesterol, mg	35		
Sodium, mg	750		

Easy Chef Salad

While chef salads can be topped with any flavor dressing, a Mexican-inspired dressing adds a fun new twist. If prepared Mexican salad dressing is not available in your area, mix ¼ teaspoon each chile powder and ground cumin into 1 cup of French dressing.

8 cups bite-size pieces mixed salad greens or 1 package (4 ounces) mixed salad greens

2 medium stalks celery, chopped (about 1 cup)

1 pint cherry tomatoes, cut in half

1 can (15 to 16 ounces) garbanzo beans, rinsed and drained

1 cup shredded mozzarella cheese (4 ounces)

¼ pound sliced cooked chicken, cut into strips

¼ pound sliced fully cooked smoked ham, cut into strips

1 cup prepared Mexican dressing

Mix salad greens, celery, tomatoes and beans in large serving bowl. Arrange cheese, chicken and ham on top. Serve with dressing. *4 servings.*

Nutrition Information Per Serving

1 serving		% of U.S. RDA	
Calories	355	Vitamin A	44%
Protein, g	32	Vitamin C	90%
Carbohydrate, g	35	Calcium	32%
Dietary fiber, g	7	Iron	30%
Fat, g	13		
Cholesterol, mg	60		
Sodium, mg	1280		

Southern Chicken Salad

(Photograph on page 93)

4 skinless boneless chicken breast halves (about 1 pound)

1 cup dry white wine or chicken broth

Buttermilk Dressing (right)

2 medium stalks celery, finely chopped (about 1 cup)

3 medium peaches, coarsely chopped, or 1 package (16 ounces) frozen sliced peaches, thawed and chopped

1 head Boston lettuce, torn into bite-size pieces

1 cup chopped pecans, toasted

Place chicken breast halves in 10-inch skillet; pour wine into skillet. Cook over medium heat 10 to 15 minutes, turning once, until juices of chicken run clear; drain. Cool chicken. Prepare Buttermilk Dressing.

Cut chicken into 1-inch pieces. Mix chicken, celery and peaches in large bowl. Add ¼ cup of the dressing; toss to coat. Cover and refrigerate 1 hour. Arrange lettuce on large serving plate. Spoon chicken mixture onto lettuce. Sprinkle with pecans. Serve with remaining dressing. *6 servings.*

BUTTERMILK DRESSING

½ cup mayonnaise or salad dressing

½ cup buttermilk

2 tablespoons chopped fresh or 2 teaspoons dried tarragon leaves

½ teaspoon salt

Shake all ingredients in tightly covered container.

Nutrition Information Per Serving

1 serving		% of U.S. RDA	
Calories	385	Vitamin A	6%
Protein, g	19	Vitamin C	10%
Carbohydrate, g	12	Calcium	6%
Dietary fiber, g	2	Iron	10%
Fat, g	30		
Cholesterol, mg	50		
Sodium, mg	370		

Cooked Poultry Yields

Use the following guidelines to determine how much uncooked chicken or turkey is needed when a recipe calls for cubed, chopped or shredded cooked chicken:

• One 2½- to 3-pound broiler-fryer chicken yields about 2½ to 3 cups.

• One and one-half pounds of whole chicken breast yields about 2 cups.

• One and one-half pounds of skinless boneless chicken breast yields about 3 cups.

• One 6- to 8-pound turkey yields about 7 to 10 cups.

EASY BREAD FIX-UPS

With a little imagination, everyday bread becomes something special with these easy bread "fix-ups." You'll love their ease and speed, as well as the finishing touch they add to your main-dish salads.

Lemon English Muffins

(Photograph on page 95)

4 English muffins, split

¼ cup (½ stick) margarine or butter, softened

1 tablespoon honey

½ teaspoon grated lemon peel

Set oven control to broil. Place muffins, cut sides up, on rack in broiler pan. Broil with tops 4 inches from heat 2 to 3 minutes or until golden brown. Mix remaining ingredients; spread on hot muffins. *4 servings.*

Nutrition Information Per Serving

1 serving		% of U.S. RDA	
Calories	240	Vitamin A	16%
Protein, g	4	Vitamin C	*
Carbohydrate, g	29	Calcium	10%
Dietary fiber, g	2	Iron	8%
Fat, g	12		
Cholesterol, mg	0		
Sodium, mg	430		

Festive Garlic Bread

(Photograph on page 87)

1-pound loaf French bread

½ cup (1 stick) margarine or butter, softened

1 tablespoon chopped fresh parsley or 1 teaspoon dried parsley flakes

¼ to ½ teaspoon garlic powder

Heat oven to 400°. Cut bread loaf into 1-inch slices without cutting through bottom of loaf. Mix remaining ingredients; spread on both sides of bread slices. Wrap bread in aluminum foil. Bake about 15 minutes or until hot. *12 servings.*

Nutrition Information Per Serving

1 serving		% of U.S. RDA	
Calories	165	Vitamin A	10%
Protein, g	3	Vitamin C	*
Carbohydrate, g	20	Calcium	4%
Dietary fiber, g	1	Iron	6%
Fat, g	8		
Cholesterol, mg	0		
Sodium, mg	310		

Italian Bread with Herb Spread

(Photograph on page 38)

8 slices Italian bread

¼ cup (½ stick) margarine or butter, softened

2 tablespoons grated Parmesan cheese

½ teaspoon Italian seasoning

Set oven control to broil. Place bread on rack in broiler pan. Broil with tops about 4 inches from heat about 2 minutes or until brown. Mix remaining ingredients; spread on untoasted sides of bread. Broil about 1½ minutes or until hot and bubbly. Cut each slice into 3 strips. *8 servings.*

Nutrition Information Per Serving

1 serving		% of U.S. RDA	
Calories	100	Vitamin A	8%
Protein, g	2	Vitamin C	*
Carbohydrate, g	10	Calcium	4%
Dietary fiber, g	1	Iron	4%
Fat, g	6		
Cholesterol, mg	0		
Sodium, mg	210		

Parmesan-Rye Fingers

3 tablespoons margarine or butter, softened

6 slices rye bread with caraway seed

3 tablespoons grated Parmesan cheese

Set oven control to broil. Spread margarine on bread. Sprinkle with cheese. Cut each slice crosswise into 4 strips. Place strips on rack in broiler pan. Broil with tops 4 inches from heat 1½ to 2 minutes or until cheese is brown. *6 servings.*

Nutrition Information Per Serving

1 serving		% of U.S. RDA	
Calories	120	Vitamin A	8%
Protein, g	3	Vitamin C	*
Carbohydrate, g	11	Calcium	6%
Dietary fiber, g	2	Iron	4%
Fat, g	7		
Cholesterol, mg	5		
Sodium, mg	290		

Toasted Bagel Rounds

3 plain bagels

¼ cup (½ stick) margarine or butter, softened

¼ teaspoon garlic powder

Dash of ground red pepper (cayenne)

Set oven control to broil. Cut each bagel horizontally into 4 slices. Mix remaining ingredients; spread on bagels. Place on ungreased cookie sheet. Broil with tops 6 inches from heat 1½ to 2 minutes or until light brown. *6 servings.*

Nutrition Information Per Serving

1 serving		% of U.S. RDA	
Calories	140	Vitamin A	10%
Protein, g	3	Vitamin C	*
Carbohydrate, g	14	Calcium	*
Dietary fiber, g	1	Iron	6%
Fat, g	8		
Cholesterol, mg	0		
Sodium, mg	200		

Turkey Taco Salad

Ground turkey makes a good lower-fat substitution for ground beef, but it is very dry. To keep the meat moist, we cooked it with a little water and seasoning, instead of adding them after the meat had browned.

1 pound ground turkey

¾ cup water

2 teaspoons chile powder

½ teaspoon salt

½ teaspoon ground cumin

1 small onion, finely chopped

1 clove garlic, finely chopped

1 can (11 ounces) whole kernel corn, drained

6 cups corn tortilla chips (about 3 ounces)

4 cups shredded iceberg lettuce

1 medium tomato, chopped (about ¾ cup)

1 cup salsa

Cook ground turkey, water, chile powder, salt, cumin, onion and garlic in 10-inch skillet over medium-high heat 10 to 12 minutes, stirring frequently, until turkey is done and liquid is absorbed. Stir in corn; cover and keep warm over low heat. Arrange tortilla chips on large serving plate. Top with lettuce, tomato, turkey mixture and salsa. Serve immediately. *4 servings.*

Nutrition Information Per Serving

1 serving		% of U.S. RDA	
Calories	480	Vitamin A	20%
Protein, g	29	Vitamin C	30%
Carbohydrate, g	49	Calcium	8%
Dietary fiber, g	5	Iron	26%
Fat, g	21		
Cholesterol, mg	80		
Sodium, mg	1560		

Turkey-Couscous Salad

This Mediterranean-inspired salad mixes the fresh, cool flavors of yogurt and mint with the salty tang of feta cheese. For a stronger, more traditionally Mediterranean flavor, look for feta cheese made with sheep's or goat's milk instead of the more common cow's milk.

1 cup uncooked couscous

½ pound sliced cooked turkey breast, cut into ½-inch strips

2 cups cherry tomatoes, cut in half

1 cup pitted ripe olives, cut in half

¾ cup plain yogurt

¼ cup chopped fresh mint leaves

2 tablespoons red wine vinegar

½ cup crumbled feta cheese

Cook couscous as directed on package. Mix couscous, turkey, tomatoes and olives in large serving bowl. Mix yogurt, mint and vinegar; stir into couscous mixture. Top with cheese. *4 servings.*

Nutrition Information Per Serving

1 serving		% of U.S. RDA	
Calories	380	Vitamin A	12%
Protein, g	28	Vitamin C	30%
Carbohydrate, g	46	Calcium	22%
Dietary fiber, g	4	Iron	18%
Fat, g	11		
Cholesterol, mg	60		
Sodium, mg	540		

Tropical Orange Roughy Salad

1 tablespoon vegetable oil

1 pound orange roughy fillets

½ cup slivered almonds

½ teaspoon ground cumin

1 small bunch romaine, torn into bite-size pieces

2 cups cubed fresh pineapple or 1 can (20 ounces) pineapple chunks in juice, drained

2 kiwifruit, peeled, cut lengthwise in half and sliced

½ cup vegetable oil

¼ cup balsamic vinegar

Heat 1 tablespoon oil in 10-inch skillet over medium-high heat. Cook fish fillets in oil 6 to 8 minutes, turning after 4 minutes, until fish flakes easily with fork. Remove fish from skillet; break into pieces. Cook almonds and cumin in same skillet about 1 minute or until almonds are toasted.

1nbPlace romaine, pineapple, kiwifruit and almonds in large serving bowl. Mix ½ cup oil and the vinegar. Add ¼ cup of the oil-and-vinegar mixture to romaine mixture; toss to coat. Add fish; gently toss. Serve immediately with remaining oil-and-vinegar mixture. *4 servings.*

Nutrition Information Per Serving

1 serving		% of U.S. RDA	
Calories	585	Vitamin A	20%
Protein, g	26	Vitamin C	100%
Carbohydrate, g	21	Calcium	12%
Dietary fiber, g	4	Iron	20%
Fat, g	46		
Cholesterol, mg	80		
Sodium, mg	70		

Salad Greens

The most successful salads are composed of fresh, dry salad greens and are often a combination of several kinds of greens—dark and pale green, crisp and tender, bland and tangy. Shredded red cabbage and fresh herbs also add welcome flavor and interest.

• Several hours before serving, wash greens thoroughly under running cold water. Shake off moisture; toss in a towel, dry in a salad spinner or blot with paper towels. Return greens to the refrigerator in a plastic bag, allowing them to regain their crispness.

• With the exception of iceberg lettuce, which can be shredded or served as lettuce cups or wedges, salad greens should be torn rather than cut into bite-size pieces.

• At serving time, pour on only enough dressing to coat all ingredients lightly; toss.

Pasta for Salads

• All cooked pasta can be used interchange-ably in salads, measure for measure. When using uncooked pasta, substitute a pasta close in shape and size or the cooked volume may vary due to weight differences.

• If pasta is to be used in a cold salad, rinse it in cold water to prevent sticking together; drain well.

• For pasta to absorb maximum flavor, add salad dressing while pasta is still warm, then refrigerate.

• Small pastas, perfect for salads: couscous, orzo (rosamarina), small shells and acini de pepe (dots).

• Medium pastas perfect for salads: fusilli (corkscrew shaped), rotelle (wagon wheels), rotini (spirals), gemelli (two pieces twisted together), radiatore (radiator shaped), farfalle (bow-ties), conchiglie (shells) and tortellini (stuffed).

• Long pastas perfect for salads: fettuccine, linguine, vermicelli and fusilli. Salads are easier to toss if you break long pastas in half or thirds before cooking.

• One ounce of uncooked pasta will yield approximately ½ cup of cooked pasta.

Tomato-Tortellini Salad

(Photograph on page 94)

We chose chicken- and cheese-filled tortellini for this recipe but one of the many other types of prepared tortellini or ravioli would also be delicious. Try Italian sausage, basil and cheese or chicken and proscuitto filling next time you make the salad.

1 package (9 ounces) refrigerated cheese-filled tortellini

1 package (9 ounces) refrigerated chicken-filled tortellini

4 cups shredded leaf lettuce

3 tablespoons chopped fresh basil leaves

2 medium tomatoes, chopped (about 1½ cups)

½ teaspoon pepper

3 tablespoons olive or vegetable oil

2 tablespoons cider vinegar

1 tablespoon Dijon mustard

Cook tortellini as directed on packages; drain. Mix lettuce, basil, tomatoes and pepper in medium bowl; stir in tortellini. Mix oil, vinegar and mustard; toss with tortellini mixture. Cover and refrigerate about 1 hour or until chilled. *6 servings.*

Nutrition Information Per Serving

1 serving		% of U.S. RDA	
Calories	240	Vitamin A	18%
Protein, g	12	Vitamin C	10%
Carbohydrate, g	19	Calcium	10%
Dietary fiber, g	2	Iron	14%
Fat, g	14		
Cholesterol, mg	110		
Sodium, mg	390		

Fettuccine-Salmon Salad

1 package (8 ounces) spinach fettuccine

1 cup refrigerated dill dip

1 package (10 ounces) frozen green peas, thawed

4 green onions, thinly sliced

1 can (14³/₄ ounces) red or pink salmon, drained, skin and bones removed, and flaked

Cook fettuccine as directed on package; drain. Toss fettuccine, ½ cup of the dill dip, the peas and onions in large serving bowl. Top with salmon. Serve immediately with remaining dill dip. *4 servings.*

Nutrition Information Per Serving

1 serving		% of U.S. RDA	
Calories	460	Vitamin A	10%
Protein, g	31	Vitamin C	4%
Carbohydrate, g	50	Calcium	30%
Dietary fiber, g	6	Iron	24%
Fat, g	18		
Cholesterol, mg	140		
Sodium, mg	1230		

Citrus Shrimp Salad

(Photograph on page 95)

Citrus Dressing (below)

1 package (12 ounces) fusilli (corkscrew shape) pasta

3 oranges, peeled and cut into sections

2 grapefruit, peeled and cut into sections

1 package (16 ounces) frozen cooked shrimp, thawed

Prepare Citrus Dressing. Cook pasta as directed on package; drain. Mix pasta and remaining ingredients in glass or plastic bowl. Toss with dressing. Cover and refrigerate about 1 hour or until chilled. *6 servings.*

CITRUS DRESSING

¹/₃ cup vegetable oil

¹/₄ cup orange juice

2 tablespoons lemon juice

2 teaspoons grated orange peel

1 teaspoon grated lemon peel

¹/₂ teaspoon salt

Shake all ingredients in tightly covered container.

Nutrition Information Per Serving

1 serving		% of U.S. RDA	
Calories	450	Vitamin A	6%
Protein, g	24	Vitamin C	100%
Carbohydrate, g	61	Calcium	8%
Dietary fiber, g	4	Iron	26%
Fat, g	14		
Cholesterol, mg	150		
Sodium, mg	570		

Black Bean Salad

(Photograph on page 96)

This south-of-the-border salad is very flexible. If yellow squash are not available, substitute a cup of whole kernel corn; chili powder can be used instead of cumin.

3 tablespoons cider vinegar

2 tablespoons vegetable oil

1 teaspoon ground cumin

½ teaspoon salt

4 cups bite-size pieces lettuce

1 cup cubed jicama

1 medium yellow summer squash, chopped

1 small red or green bell pepper, chopped (about ½ cup)

2 cans (15 ounces each) black beans, rinsed and drained

Mix vinegar, oil, cumin and salt in large serving bowl. Add remaining ingredients; toss. *6 servings.*

Nutrition Information Per Serving

1 serving		% of U.S. RDA	
Calories	175	Vitamin A	10%
Protein, g	10	Vitamin C	40%
Carbohydrate, g	31	Calcium	10%
Dietary fiber, g	8	Iron	18%
Fat, g	5		
Cholesterol, mg	0		
Sodium, mg	420		

Spicy Seafood Salad

1 cup uncooked regular long grain rice

½ cup spicy eight-vegetable juice

½ teaspoon salt

2 medium stalks celery, chopped (about 1 cup)

2 medium tomatoes, chopped (about 1½ cups)

1 medium red bell pepper, chopped (about 1 cup)

1 package (8 ounces) frozen salad-style imitation crabmeat, thawed

1 package (8 ounces) frozen cooked shrimp, thawed

Cook rice as directed on package. Mix rice and remaining ingredients in large serving bowl. Cover and refrigerate about 1 hour or until chilled. *4 servings.*

Nutrition Information Per Serving

1 serving		% of U.S. RDA	
Calories	310	Vitamin A	22%
Protein, g	25	Vitamin C	90%
Carbohydrate, g	50	Calcium	6%
Dietary fiber, g	2	Iron	22%
Fat, g	2		
Cholesterol, mg	130		
Sodium, mg	1570		

Hawaiian Crab Salad

Papaya and mango, both tropical fruits that have become more readily available throughout this country, have sweet, fresh flavors when ripe. Use a grapefruit spoon to scoop out the seeds from the papaya. Take a knife and carefully cut away the mango pulp from the large, flat pit in the middle of the fruit.

1 cup fresh or frozen raspberries

1 medium bunch leaf lettuce, coarsely shredded

1 papaya, peeled, seeded and chopped

1 mango, peeled, pitted and chopped

2 packages (8 ounces each) frozen salad-style imitation crabmeat, thawed

Raspberry Vinaigrette (right)

¹/₄ cup chopped macadamia nuts

Mix all ingredients except Raspberry Vinaigrette and nuts in large serving bowl. Toss with vinaigrette. Sprinkle with nuts. *4 servings.*

RASPBERRY VINAIGRETTE

¹/₄ cup vegetable oil

2 tablespoons raspberry vinegar

2 teaspoons raspberry jam

Shake all ingredients in tightly covered container.

Nutrition Information Per Serving

1 serving		% of U.S. RDA	
Calories	365	Vitamin A	38%
Protein, g	19	Vitamin C	100%
Carbohydrate, g	32	Calcium	6%
Dietary fiber, g	5	Iron	8%
Fat, g	20		
Cholesterol, mg	35		
Sodium, mg	1010		

METRIC CONVERSION GUIDE

U.S. UNITS	CANADIAN METRIC	AUSTRALIAN METRIC
Volume		
1/4 teaspoon	1 mL	1 ml
1/2 teaspoon	2 mL	2 ml
1 teaspoon	5 mL	5 ml
1 tablespoon	15 mL	20 ml
1/4 cup	50 mL	60 ml
1/3 cup	75 mL	80 ml
1/2 cup	125 mL	125 ml
2/3 cup	150 mL	170 ml
3/4 cup	175 mL	190 ml
1 cup	250 mL	250 ml
1 quart	1 liter	1 liter
1 1/2 quarts	1.5 liter	1.5 liter
2 quarts	2 liters	2 liters
2 1/2 quarts	2.5 liters	2.5 liters
3 quarts	3 liters	3 liters
4 quarts	4 liters	4 liters
Weight		
1 ounce	30 grams	30 grams
2 ounces	55 grams	60 grams
3 ounces	85 grams	90 grams
4 ounces (1/4 pound)	115 grams	125 grams
8 ounces (1/2 pound)	225 grams	225 grams
16 ounces (1 pound)	455 grams	500 grams
1 pound	455 grams	1/2 kilogram

Measurements		**Temperatures**	
Inches	Centimeters	Fahrenheit	Celsius
1	2.5	32°	0°
2	5.0	212°	100°
3	7.5	250°	120°
4	10.0	275°	140°
5	12.5	300°	150°
6	15.0	325°	160°
7	17.5	350°	180°
8	20.5	375°	190°
9	23.0	400°	200°
10	25.5	425°	220°
11	28.0	450°	230°
12	30.5	475°	240°
13	33.0	500°	260°
14	35.5		
15	38.0		

NOTE
The recipes in this cookbook have not been developed or tested using metric measures. When converting recipes to metric, some variations in quality may be noted.

INDEX

Page numbers in *italics* indicate photographs.

Betty Crocker
50 POINTS
SAVE these Betty Crocker Points and redeem them for big savings on hundreds of kitchen, home, gift and children's items! For catalog, send 50¢ with your name and address to: General Mills, P.O. Box 5389 Mpls., MN 55460.
Redeemable with cash in USA before May 1999.
Void where prohibited, taxed or regulated.
S
CUT OUT AND SAVE